CONFIGURING SALES ORDER MANAGEMENT WITHIN DYNAMICS 365 FOR FINANCE & OPERATIONS

MODULE 1: CONFIGURING SALES ORDER MANAGEMENT CONTROLS

MURRAY FIFE

ISBN-13: 978-1078200783

Preface

What You Need for this Guide

All the examples shown in this blueprint were done with the Microsoft Dynamics 365 for Operations hosted image that was provisioned through Lifecycle Services.

The following list of software from the virtual image was leveraged within this guide:

Microsoft Dynamics 365 for Operations

Even though all the preceding software was used during the development and testing of the recipes in this book, they should also work on later versions without any changes.

Errata

Although we have taken every care to ensure the accuracy of our content, mistakes do happen. If you find a mistake in one of our books—may be a mistake in the text or the code—we would be grateful if you would report this to us. By doing so, you can save other readers from frustration and help us improve subsequent versions of this book. If you find any errata, please report them by emailing editor@dynamicscompanions.com.

Piracy

Piracy of copyright material on the Internet is an ongoing problem across all media. If you come across any illegal copies of our works, in any form, on the Internet, please provide us with the location address or website name immediately so that we can pursue a remedy.

Please contact us at legal@dynamicscompanions.com with a link to the suspected pirated material.

We appreciate your help in protecting our authors and our ability to bring you valuable content.

Questions

You can contact us at help@dynamicscompanions.com if you are having a problem with any aspect of the book, and we will do our best to address it.

Table of Contents

DYNAMICS COMPANIONS
BARE BONES CONFIGURATION GUIDE

CONFIGURING SALES ORDER MANAGEMENT WITHIN DYNAMICS 365 FOR FINANCE & OPERATIONS
MODULE 1: CONFIGURING SALES ORDER MANAGEMENT CONTROLS

Configuring Sales Order Management Controls

Before we start taking Sales Orders there are a few codes and controls that we need to set up to make our life a little easier. Some of these include the configuration of codes to be used within the orders themselves like the **Sales Origin**, **Delivery Terms**, and **Modes of Delivery**, and others are just configurations that will make you order entry process even easier. Like the **Order Search** feature and the **Event Tracking** feature.

Topics Covered

- Configuring the Accounts Receivable Parameters for Sales Order Management

- Configuring Customer Reason Codes

- Configuring Delivery Terms

- Configuring Modes Of Delivery

- Configuring Sales Order Origin Codes

- Enabling Order Event Tracking

- Configuring Order Search Parameters

www.dynamicscompanions.com
Dynamics Companions

- 7 -

www.blindsquirrelpublishing.com
© 2019 Blind Squirrel Publishing, LLC , All Rights Reserved

BLIND SQUIRREL
PUBLISHING

DYNAMICS COMPANIONS
BARE BONES CONFIGURATION GUIDE

CONFIGURING SALES ORDER MANAGEMENT WITHIN DYNAMICS 365 FOR FINANCE & OPERATIONS
MODULE 1: CONFIGURING SALES ORDER MANAGEMENT CONTROLS

Configuring the Accounts Receivable Parameters for Sales Order Management

The very first thing that we need to do though is to make a small tweak to the **Accounts Receivable** parameters, so that we can create Sales Orders, and also so that the system will track our prices and discounts on the sales order.

Topics Covered

- Opening the Accounts Receivable Parameters form

- Changing the default Journal type to Sales Orders

- Updating the Pricing default parameters

- Review

dyn c
www.dynamicscompanions.com
Dynamics Companions

- 8 -

www.blindsquirrelpublishing.com
© 2019 Blind Squirrel Publishing, LLC , All Rights Reserved

BLIND SQUIRREL PUBLISHING

DYNAMICS COMPANIONS
BARE BONES CONFIGURATION GUIDE

CONFIGURING SALES ORDER MANAGEMENT WITHIN DYNAMICS 365 FOR FINANCE & OPERATIONS
MODULE 1: CONFIGURING SALES ORDER MANAGEMENT CONTROLS

Opening the Accounts Receivable Parameters form

In order to do this we will want to start off by finding the form that we can use to set up all of our Sales Order parameters.

How to do it...

Step 1: Open the Accounts receivable parameters form through the menu

We can get to the **Accounts receivable parameters** form a couple of different ways. The first way is through the master menu.

Navigate to Accounts Receivable > Setup > Accounts receivable parameters.

Step 2: Open the Accounts receivable parameters form through the menu search

Another way that we can find the **Accounts receivable parameters** form is through the menu search feature.

Type in **accounts r p** into the menu search and select **Accounts receivable parameters**.

dyn c
www.dynamicscompanions.com
Dynamics Companions

- 9 -

www.blindsquirrelpublishing.com
© 2019 Blind Squirrel Publishing, LLC , All Rights Reserved

BLIND SQUIRREL
PUBLISHING

DYNAMICS COMPANIONS
BARE BONES CONFIGURATION GUIDE

CONFIGURING SALES ORDER MANAGEMENT WITHIN DYNAMICS 365 FOR FINANCE & OPERATIONS
MODULE 1: CONFIGURING SALES ORDER MANAGEMENT CONTROLS

Opening the Accounts Receivable Parameters form

How to do it...

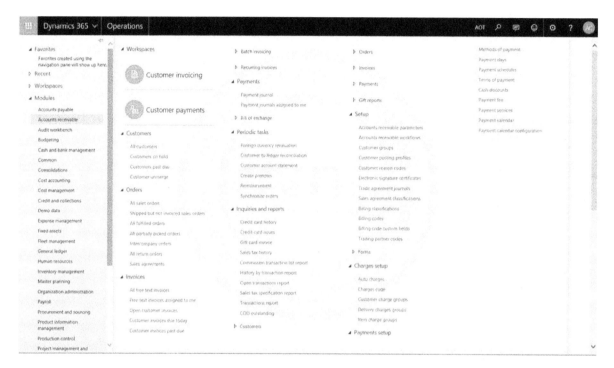

Step 1: Open the Accounts receivable parameters form through the menu

We can get to the **Accounts receivable parameters** form a couple of different ways. The first way is through the master menu.

In order to do this, open up the navigation panel, expand out the **Modules** and group, and click on **Accounts Receivable** to see all of the menu items that are available. Then click on the **Accounts receivable parameters** menu item within the **Setup** group.

dyn c
www.dynamicscompanions.com
Dynamics Companions

- 10 -

www.blindsquirrelpublishing.com
© 2019 Blind Squirrel Publishing, LLC, All Rights Reserved

BLIND SQUIRREL
PUBLISHING

DYNAMICS COMPANIONS
BARE BONES CONFIGURATION GUIDE

CONFIGURING SALES ORDER MANAGEMENT WITHIN DYNAMICS 365 FOR FINANCE & OPERATIONS
MODULE 1: CONFIGURING SALES ORDER MANAGEMENT CONTROLS

Opening the Accounts Receivable Parameters form

How to do it...

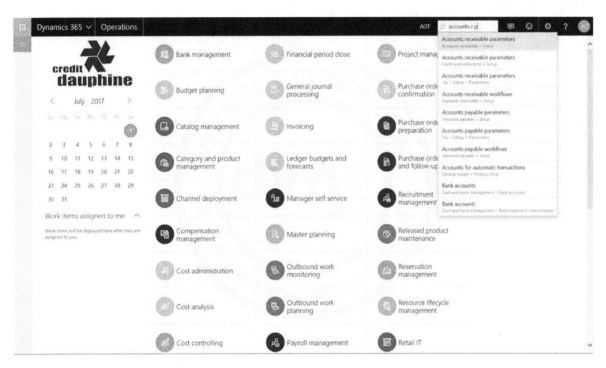

Step 2: Open the Accounts receivable parameters form through the menu search

Another way that we can find the **Accounts receivable parameters** form is through the menu search feature.

We can do this by clicking on the search icon in the header of the form (or by pressing **ALT+G**) and then type in **accounts r p** into the search box. Then you will be able to select the **Accounts receivable parameters** form from the dropdown list.

dync
www.dynamicscompanions.com
Dynamics Companions
- 11 -
www.blindsquirrelpublishing.com
© 2019 Blind Squirrel Publishing, LLC , All Rights Reserved
BLIND SQUIRREL
PUBLISHING

DYNAMICS COMPANIONS
BARE BONES CONFIGURATION GUIDE

CONFIGURING SALES ORDER MANAGEMENT WITHIN DYNAMICS 365 FOR FINANCE & OPERATIONS
MODULE 1: CONFIGURING SALES ORDER MANAGEMENT CONTROLS

Opening the Accounts Receivable Parameters form

How to do it...

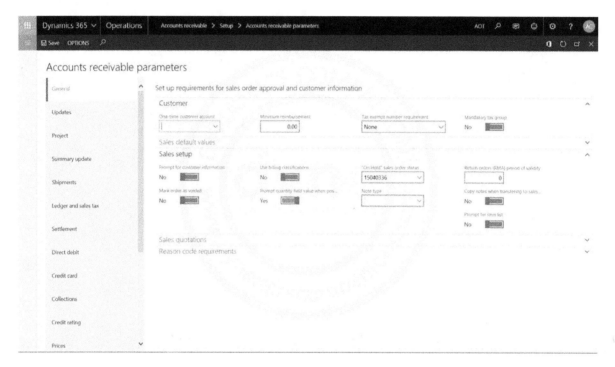

Step 2: Open the Accounts receivable parameters form through the menu search

This will open up the Accounts receivable parameters maintenance form where we will be able to tweak some of the different parameters that are associated with the Sales order processing functions.

www.dynamicscompanions.com
Dynamics Companions

- 12 -

www.blindsquirrelpublishing.com
© 2019 Blind Squirrel Publishing, LLC , All Rights Reserved

BLIND SQUIRREL
PUBLISHING

DYNAMICS COMPANIONS
BARE BONES CONFIGURATION GUIDE

CONFIGURING SALES ORDER MANAGEMENT WITHIN DYNAMICS 365 FOR FINANCE & OPERATIONS
MODULE 1: CONFIGURING SALES ORDER MANAGEMENT CONTROLS

Changing the default Journal type to Sales Orders

Now that we are within the Accounts receivable parameters we will want to make a couple of changes to the default parameters.

We will start off by changing the default journal type that is used when a Sales order is created.

How to do it...

Step 1: Click on the General page group

If when the **Accounts receivable parameters** form is displayed, you are not on the **General** tab then we will want to switch to it.

Click on the **General** page group.

Step 2: Click on the Sales order defaults button

Next we will want to look at all of the defaults for Sales order processing.

Click on the **Sales order defaults** button.

Step 3: Select the Order type

By default, the system is configured so that when we create a sale order, it creates a Journal. For us, this is not the most useful configuration, because Journals do not require products to be picked or shipped.

So we will want to change the configuration so that when we create a Sales order, then it creates an order of type **Sales order** which includes the option to pick and ship the products.

Click on the **Order type** dropdown list And choose **Sales order**.

 www.dynamicscompanions.com
Dynamics Companions

- 13 -

www.blindsquirrelpublishing.com
© 2019 Blind Squirrel Publishing, LLC, All Rights Reserved

BLIND SQUIRREL
PUBLISHING

DYNAMICS COMPANIONS
BARE BONES CONFIGURATION GUIDE

CONFIGURING SALES ORDER MANAGEMENT WITHIN DYNAMICS 365 FOR FINANCE & OPERATIONS
MODULE 1: CONFIGURING SALES ORDER MANAGEMENT CONTROLS

Changing the default Journal type to Sales Orders

How to do it...

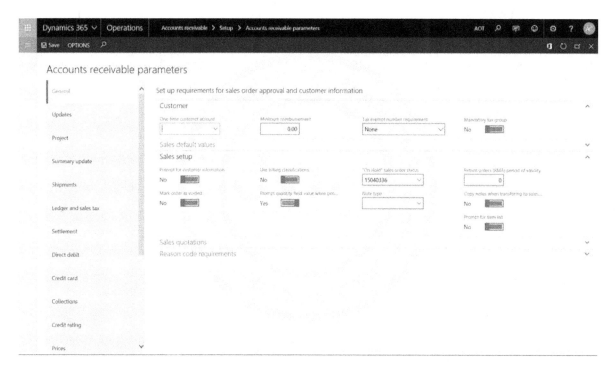

Step 1: Click on the General page group

If when the **Accounts receivable parameters** form is displayed, you are not on the **General** tab then we will want to switch to it.

To do this all we need to do is click on the **General** page group.

dync
www.dynamicscompanions.com
Dynamics Companions

- 14 -

www.blindsquirrelpublishing.com
© 2019 Blind Squirrel Publishing, LLC , All Rights Reserved

BLIND SQUIRREL
PUBLISHING

DYNAMICS COMPANIONS
BARE BONES CONFIGURATION GUIDE

CONFIGURING SALES ORDER MANAGEMENT WITHIN DYNAMICS 365 FOR FINANCE & OPERATIONS
MODULE 1: CONFIGURING SALES ORDER MANAGEMENT CONTROLS

Changing the default Journal type to Sales Orders

How to do it...

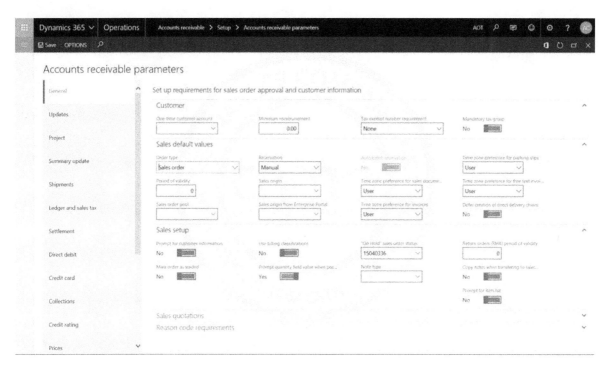

Step 2: Click on the Sales order defaults button

Next we will want to look at all of the defaults for Sales order processing.

To do this all we need to do is click on the **Sales order defaults** button.

dyn c

www.dynamicscompanions.com
Dynamics Companions

- 15 -

www.blindsquirrelpublishing.com
© 2019 Blind Squirrel Publishing, LLC , All Rights Reserved

BLIND SQUIRREL
PUBLISHING

DYNAMICS COMPANIONS
BARE BONES CONFIGURATION GUIDE

CONFIGURING SALES ORDER MANAGEMENT WITHIN DYNAMICS 365 FOR FINANCE & OPERATIONS
MODULE 1: CONFIGURING SALES ORDER MANAGEMENT CONTROLS

Changing the default Journal type to Sales Orders

How to do it...

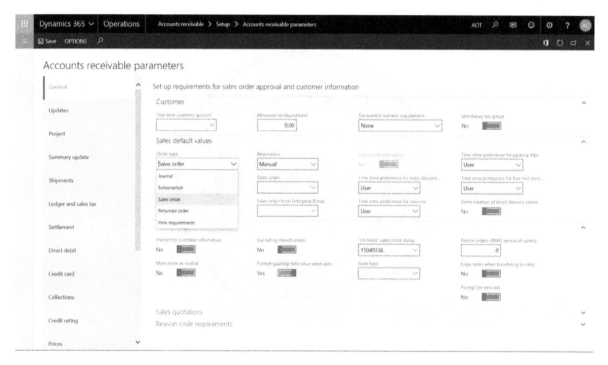

Step 3: Select the Order type

By default, the system is configured so that when we create a sale order, it creates a Journal. For us, this is not the most useful configuration, because Journals do not require products to be picked or shipped.

So we will want to change the configuration so that when we create a Sales order, then it creates an order of type **Sales order** which includes the option to pick and ship the products.

To do this just select the **Order type** value from the dropdown list.

This time, we will want to click on the **Order type** dropdown list and select **Sales order**.

dync
www.dynamicscompanions.com
Dynamics Companions

- 16 -

www.blindsquirrelpublishing.com
© 2019 Blind Squirrel Publishing, LLC , All Rights Reserved

BLIND SQUIRREL
PUBLISHING

DYNAMICS COMPANIONS
BARE BONES CONFIGURATION GUIDE

CONFIGURING SALES ORDER MANAGEMENT WITHIN DYNAMICS 365 FOR FINANCE & OPERATIONS
MODULE 1: CONFIGURING SALES ORDER MANAGEMENT CONTROLS

Updating the Pricing default parameters

Next we will want to update some of the default values with respect to the pricing.

How to do it...

Step 1: Click on the Prices page group

Click on the **Prices** page group.

Step 2: Change the Find auto charges for header

We will want the system to find any automatic charges that we have set up at the header level of the sales orders.

Toggle the **Find auto charges for header** switch And make it **Yes**.

Step 3: Change the Find auto charges for line

Also, we will want to have the system find any automatic charges that we have defined at the line level as well.

Change the **Find auto charges for line** switch And make it **Yes**.

Step 4: Expand Generic currency and smart rounding tab

Next we will want to tweak some of the setting related to the currency and smart rounding options within the application.

Expand the Generic currency and smart rounding tab.

Step 5: Select the Generic currency

We will want to set a default (or generic) currency that we will use.

Click on the **Generic currency** dropdown list And choose **USD**.

Step 6: Select the Exchange rate type

Next we will want to select the currency exchange rate that you want to use in the case that prices are maintained in different currencies.

Click on the **Exchange rate type** dropdown list And select **Default**.

Step 7: Change the Apply smart rounding after currency

And also we will want to specify when we do use the smart rounding, which will round on the final number. We need to specify if we want to do this before or after the currency conversion.

Toggle the Apply smart rounding after currency switch And make it Yes.

Step 8: Expand Total discounts tab

We will want to make one last tweak to the settings within the Prices tab, and that will be related to the total discounts.

 www.dynamicscompanions.com
Dynamics Companions

- 17 -

www.blindsquirrelpublishing.com
© 2019 Blind Squirrel Publishing, LLC , All Rights Reserved

BLIND SQUIRREL
PUBLISHING

DYNAMICS COMPANIONS
BARE BONES CONFIGURATION GUIDE

CONFIGURING SALES ORDER MANAGEMENT WITHIN DYNAMICS 365 FOR FINANCE & OPERATIONS
MODULE 1: CONFIGURING SALES ORDER MANAGEMENT CONTROLS

Expand the **Total discounts** tab.

Step 9: Change the Calculate total discount at posting

In this option group we will be able to specify when the total discounts will be calculated within the order process.

Toggle the Calculate total discount at posting switch And make it Yes.

Step 10: Expand Price details tab

We will make one final change to the parameters so that we can see all of the price details, and we will make this change within the Price details tab.

Expand the **Price details** tab.

Step 11: Toggle the Enable price details

Here we will see that we have an option that allows us to see (or not see) the price details showing how the price is being built up as we are building our sales order lines.

Change the **Enable price details** switch And set it to **Yes**.

dyn c
www.dynamicscompanions.com
Dynamics Companions

- 18 -

www.blindsquirrelpublishing.com
© 2019 Blind Squirrel Publishing, LLC, All Rights Reserved

BLIND SQUIRREL
PUBLISHING

DYNAMICS COMPANIONS
BARE BONES CONFIGURATION GUIDE

CONFIGURING SALES ORDER MANAGEMENT WITHIN DYNAMICS 365 FOR FINANCE & OPERATIONS
MODULE 1: CONFIGURING SALES ORDER MANAGEMENT CONTROLS

Updating the Pricing default parameters

How to do it...

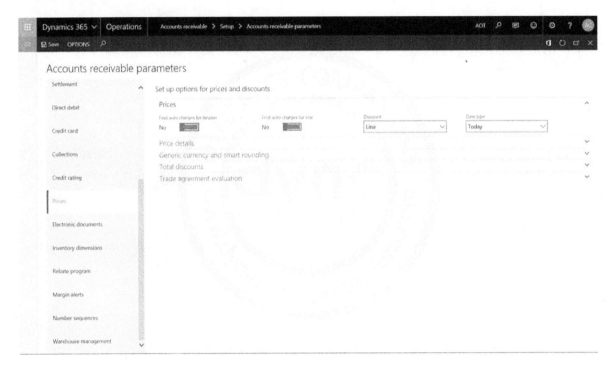

Step 1: Click on the Prices page group

To do this just click on the **Prices** page group.

dyn c
www.dynamicscompanions.com
Dynamics Companions

- 19 -

www.blindsquirrelpublishing.com
© 2019 Blind Squirrel Publishing, LLC , All Rights Reserved

BLIND SQUIRREL
PUBLISHING

DYNAMICS COMPANIONS
BARE BONES CONFIGURATION GUIDE

CONFIGURING SALES ORDER MANAGEMENT WITHIN DYNAMICS 365 FOR FINANCE & OPERATIONS
MODULE 1: CONFIGURING SALES ORDER MANAGEMENT CONTROLS

Updating the Pricing default parameters

How to do it...

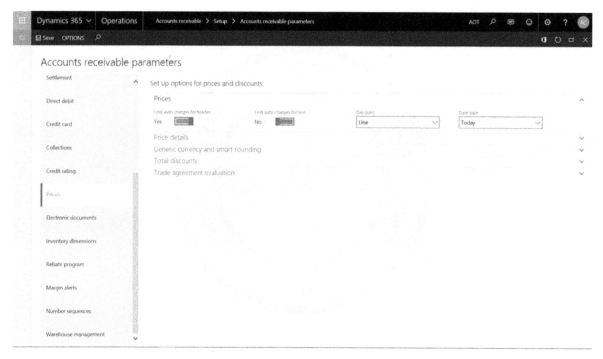

Step 2: Change the Find auto charges for header

We will want the system to find any automatic charges that we have set up at the header level of the sales orders.

To do this we will just need to toggle the **Find auto charges for header** option.

For this example, we will want to click on the **Find auto charges for header** toggle switch and update it to the **Yes** value.

dyn c
www.dynamicscompanions.com
Dynamics Companions

www.blindsquirrelpublishing.com
© 2019 Blind Squirrel Publishing, LLC , All Rights Reserved

BLIND SQUIRREL
PUBLISHING

DYNAMICS COMPANIONS
BARE BONES CONFIGURATION GUIDE

CONFIGURING SALES ORDER MANAGEMENT WITHIN DYNAMICS 365 FOR FINANCE & OPERATIONS
MODULE 1: CONFIGURING SALES ORDER MANAGEMENT CONTROLS

Updating the Pricing default parameters

How to do it...

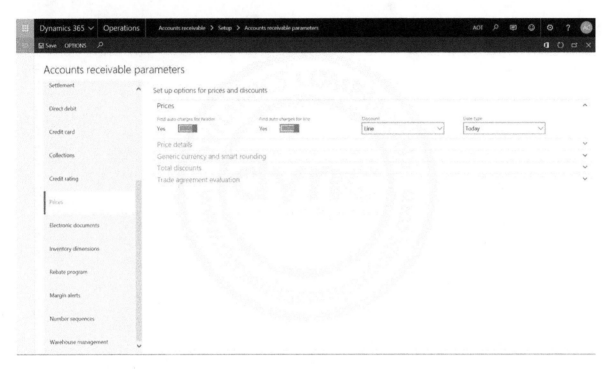

Step 3: Change the Find auto charges for line

Also, we will want to have the system find any automatic charges that we have defined at the line level as well.

To do this we will just need to change the **Find auto charges for line** option.

For this example, we will want to click on the **Find auto charges for line** toggle switch and set it to the **Yes** value.

dync
www.dynamicscompanions.com
Dynamics Companions

- 21 -

www.blindsquirrelpublishing.com
© 2019 Blind Squirrel Publishing, LLC , All Rights Reserved

BLIND SQUIRREL
PUBLISHING

DYNAMICS COMPANIONS
BARE BONES CONFIGURATION GUIDE

CONFIGURING SALES ORDER MANAGEMENT WITHIN DYNAMICS 365 FOR FINANCE & OPERATIONS
MODULE 1: CONFIGURING SALES ORDER MANAGEMENT CONTROLS

Updating the Pricing default parameters

How to do it...

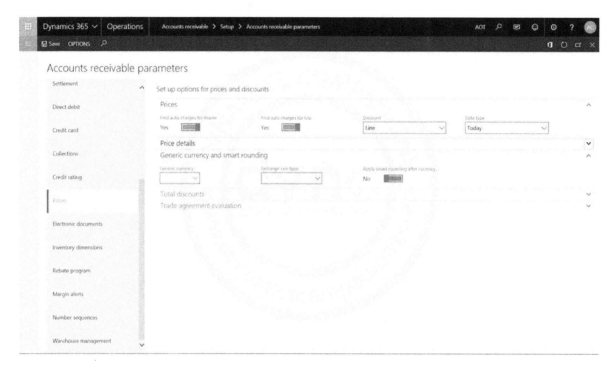

Step 4: Expand Generic currency and smart rounding tab

Next we will want to tweak some of the setting related to the currency and smart rounding options within the application.

To do this just expand the Generic currency and smart rounding tab.

dyn c
www.dynamicscompanions.com
Dynamics Companions

- 22 -

www.blindsquirrelpublishing.com
© 2019 Blind Squirrel Publishing, LLC , All Rights Reserved

BLIND SQUIRREL
PUBLISHING

DYNAMICS COMPANIONS
BARE BONES CONFIGURATION GUIDE

CONFIGURING SALES ORDER MANAGEMENT WITHIN DYNAMICS 365 FOR FINANCE & OPERATIONS
MODULE 1: CONFIGURING SALES ORDER MANAGEMENT CONTROLS

Updating the Pricing default parameters

How to do it...

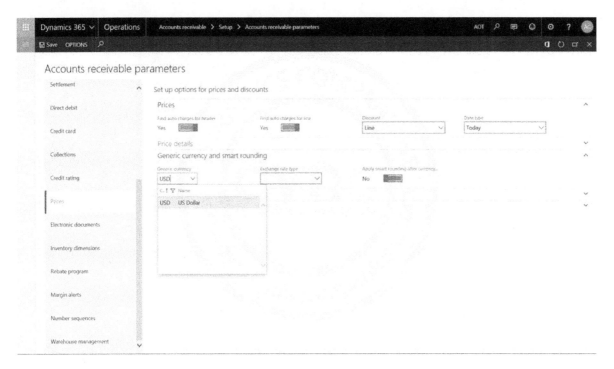

Step 5: Select the Generic currency

We will want to set a default (or generic) currency that we will use.

To do this we will just need to select the **Generic currency** value from the dropdown list.

For this example, we will want to click on the **Generic currency** dropdown list and pick **USD**.

dyn c
www.dynamicscompanions.com
Dynamics Companions

- 23 -

www.blindsquirrelpublishing.com
© 2019 Blind Squirrel Publishing, LLC , All Rights Reserved

BLIND SQUIRREL
PUBLISHING

DYNAMICS COMPANIONS
BARE BONES CONFIGURATION GUIDE

CONFIGURING SALES ORDER MANAGEMENT WITHIN DYNAMICS 365 FOR FINANCE & OPERATIONS
MODULE 1: CONFIGURING SALES ORDER MANAGEMENT CONTROLS

Updating the Pricing default parameters

How to do it...

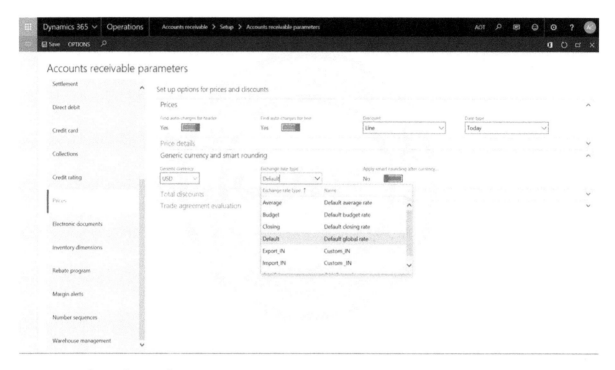

Step 6: Select the Exchange rate type

Next we will want to select the currency exchange rate that you want to use in the case that prices are maintained in different currencies.

To do this we will just need to select the **Exchange rate type** option from the dropdown list.

This time, we will want to click on the **Exchange rate type** dropdown list and select **Default**.

dync
www.dynamicscompanions.com
Dynamics Companions

- 24 -

www.blindsquirrelpublishing.com
© 2019 Blind Squirrel Publishing, LLC , All Rights Reserved

BLIND SQUIRREL
PUBLISHING

DYNAMICS COMPANIONS
BARE BONES CONFIGURATION GUIDE

CONFIGURING SALES ORDER MANAGEMENT WITHIN DYNAMICS 365 FOR FINANCE & OPERATIONS
MODULE 1: CONFIGURING SALES ORDER MANAGEMENT CONTROLS

Updating the Pricing default parameters

How to do it...

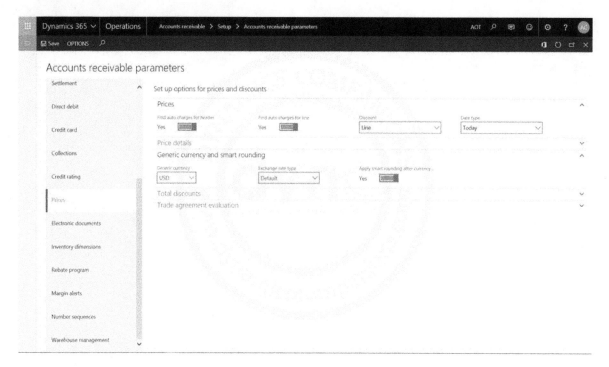

Step 7: Change the Apply smart rounding after currency

And also we will want to specify when we do use the smart rounding, which will round on the final number. We need to specify if we want to do this before or after the currency conversion.

To do this just switch the Apply smart rounding after currency value.

This time, we will want to click on the **Apply smart rounding after currency** toggle switch and change it to the **Yes** value.

dyn companions
www.dynamicscompanions.com
Dynamics Companions

- 25 -

www.blindsquirrelpublishing.com
© 2019 Blind Squirrel Publishing, LLC , All Rights Reserved

BLIND SQUIRREL
PUBLISHING

DYNAMICS COMPANIONS
BARE BONES CONFIGURATION GUIDE

CONFIGURING SALES ORDER MANAGEMENT WITHIN DYNAMICS 365 FOR FINANCE & OPERATIONS
MODULE 1: CONFIGURING SALES ORDER MANAGEMENT CONTROLS

Updating the Pricing default parameters

How to do it...

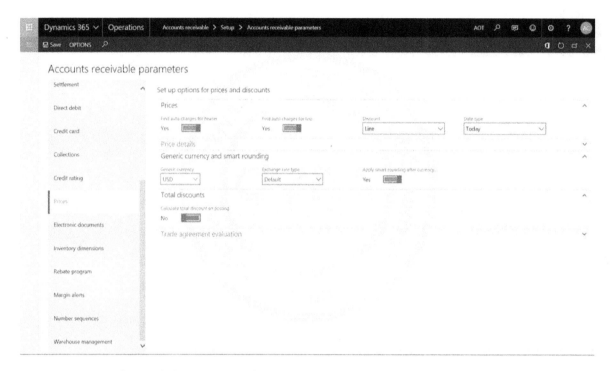

Step 8: Expand Total discounts tab

We will want to make one last tweak to the settings within the Prices tab, and that will be related to the total discounts.

To do this all we need to do is expand the **Total discounts** tab.

dyn c
www.dynamicscompanions.com
Dynamics Companions

- 26 -

www.blindsquirrelpublishing.com
© 2019 Blind Squirrel Publishing, LLC , All Rights Reserved

BLIND SQUIRREL
PUBLISHING

DYNAMICS COMPANIONS
BARE BONES CONFIGURATION GUIDE

CONFIGURING SALES ORDER MANAGEMENT WITHIN DYNAMICS 365 FOR FINANCE & OPERATIONS
MODULE 1: CONFIGURING SALES ORDER MANAGEMENT CONTROLS

Updating the Pricing default parameters

How to do it...

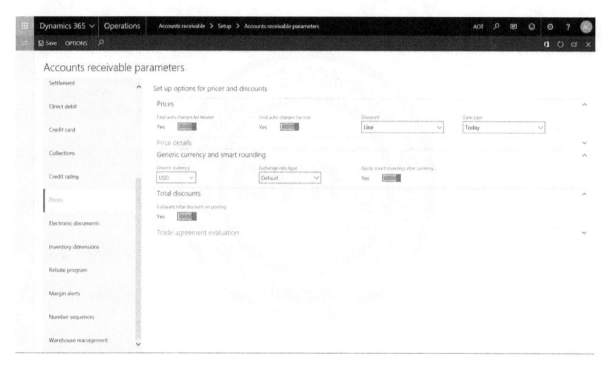

Step 9: Change the Calculate total discount at posting

In this option group we will be able to specify when the total discounts will be calculated within the order process.

To do this we will just need to change the **Calculate total discount at posting** value.

For this example, we will want to click on the **Calculate total discount at posting** toggle switch and set it to the **Yes** value.

www.dynamicscompanions.com
Dynamics Companions

- 27 -

www.blindsquirrelpublishing.com
© 2019 Blind Squirrel Publishing, LLC , All Rights Reserved

BLIND SQUIRREL
PUBLISHING

DYNAMICS COMPANIONS
BARE BONES CONFIGURATION GUIDE

CONFIGURING SALES ORDER MANAGEMENT WITHIN DYNAMICS 365 FOR FINANCE & OPERATIONS
MODULE 1: CONFIGURING SALES ORDER MANAGEMENT CONTROLS

Updating the Pricing default parameters

How to do it...

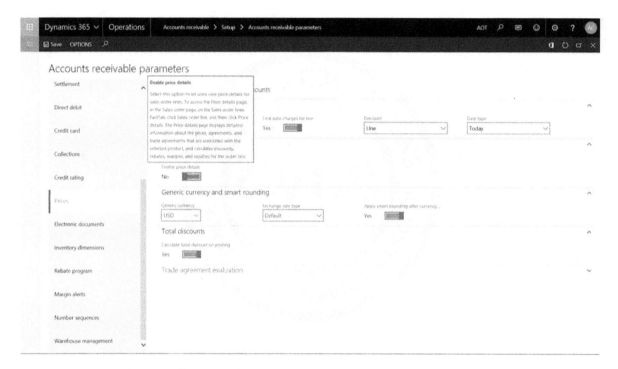

Step 10: Expand Price details tab

We will make one final change to the parameters so that we can see all of the price details, and we will make this change within the Price details tab.

To do this all we need to do is expand the **Price details** tab.

dyn c
dynamics companion
www.dynamicscompanions.com
Dynamics Companions

- 28 -

www.blindsquirrelpublishing.com
© 2019 Blind Squirrel Publishing, LLC , All Rights Reserved

BLIND SQUIRREL
PUBLISHING

DYNAMICS COMPANIONS
BARE BONES CONFIGURATION GUIDE

CONFIGURING SALES ORDER MANAGEMENT WITHIN DYNAMICS 365 FOR FINANCE & OPERATIONS
MODULE 1: CONFIGURING SALES ORDER MANAGEMENT CONTROLS

Updating the Pricing default parameters

How to do it...

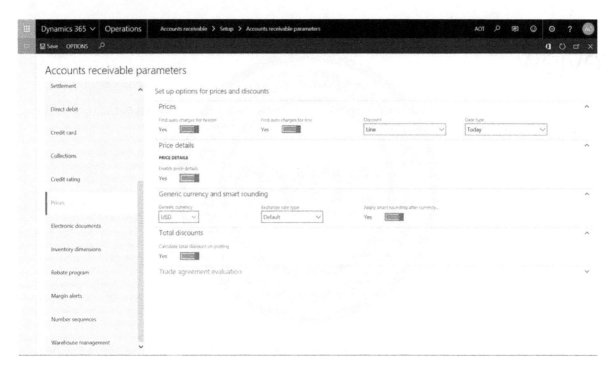

Step 11: Toggle the Enable price details

Here we will see that we have an option that allows us to see (or not see) the price details showing how the price is being built up as we are building our sales order lines.

To do this we will just need to switch the **Enable price details** value.

This time, we will want to click on the **Enable price details** toggle switch and change it to the **Yes** value.

Once you have made these small tweaks, we can exit out of the form.

dyn c

www.dynamicscompanions.com
Dynamics Companions

- 29 -

www.blindsquirrelpublishing.com
© 2019 Blind Squirrel Publishing, LLC , All Rights Reserved

BLIND SQUIRREL
PUBLISHING

DYNAMICS COMPANIONS
BARE BONES CONFIGURATION GUIDE

CONFIGURING SALES ORDER MANAGEMENT WITHIN DYNAMICS 365 FOR FINANCE & OPERATIONS
MODULE 1: CONFIGURING SALES ORDER MANAGEMENT CONTROLS

Review

Congratulations. You have now made all of the changes that we will need to the Accounts receivable parameters so that we will be able to get all of the other exercises to post correctly.

www.dynamicscompanions.com
Dynamics Companions

- 30 -

www.blindsquirrelpublishing.com
© 2019 Blind Squirrel Publishing, LLC, All Rights Reserved

BLIND SQUIRREL
PUBLISHING

DYNAMICS COMPANIONS
BARE BONES CONFIGURATION GUIDE

CONFIGURING SALES ORDER MANAGEMENT WITHIN DYNAMICS 365 FOR FINANCE & OPERATIONS
MODULE 1: CONFIGURING SALES ORDER MANAGEMENT CONTROLS

Configuring Customer Reason Codes

Next we will want to set up a few additional reason codes which we will be able to use within the Order Management process.

Topics Covered

- Opening the Customer Reasons maintenance form

- Selecting Existing Reason Codes

- Creating a Price Change Reason Code

- Creating a Quality Reason Code

- Review

www.dynamicscompanions.com
Dynamics Companions

- 31 -

www.blindsquirrelpublishing.com
© 2019 Blind Squirrel Publishing, LLC, All Rights Reserved

BLIND SQUIRREL
PUBLISHING

DYNAMICS COMPANIONS
BARE BONES CONFIGURATION GUIDE

CONFIGURING SALES ORDER MANAGEMENT WITHIN DYNAMICS 365 FOR FINANCE & OPERATIONS
MODULE 1: CONFIGURING SALES ORDER MANAGEMENT CONTROLS

Opening the Customer Reasons maintenance form

We will start off by opening up the form that will allow us to maintain all of the customer reason codes.

How to do it...

Step 1: Open the Customer reason codes form through the menu

We can get to the **Customer reason codes** form a couple of different ways. The first way is through the master menu.

Navigate to Accounts receivable > Setup > Customer reason codes.

Step 2: Open the Customer reason codes form through the menu search

Another way that we can find the **Customer reason codes** form is through the menu search feature.

Type in **cust re** into the menu search and select **Customer reason codes**.

When the **Customer Reasons** maintenance form is displayed, you will notice that there are existing reason codes that have been entered in during the setup of the other modules.

You will notice that there are existing reason codes that have been entered in during the setup of the other modules. Now we can add some more for the Sales Order Processing.

DYNAMICS COMPANIONS
BARE BONES CONFIGURATION GUIDE

CONFIGURING SALES ORDER MANAGEMENT WITHIN DYNAMICS 365 FOR FINANCE & OPERATIONS
MODULE 1: CONFIGURING SALES ORDER MANAGEMENT CONTROLS

Opening the Customer Reasons maintenance form

How to do it...

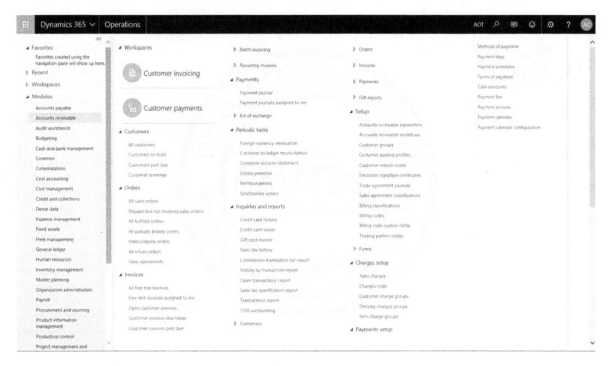

Step 1: Open the Customer reason codes form through the menu

We can get to the **Customer reason codes** form a couple of different ways. The first way is through the master menu.

To do this, open up the navigation panel, expand out the **Modules** and group, and click on **Accounts receivable** to see all of the menu items that are available. Then click on the **Customer reason codes** menu item within the **Setup** group.

dyn c
www.dynamicscompanions.com
Dynamics Companions

- 33 -

www.blindsquirrelpublishing.com
© 2019 Blind Squirrel Publishing, LLC , All Rights Reserved

BLIND SQUIRREL
PUBLISHING

DYNAMICS COMPANIONS
BARE BONES CONFIGURATION GUIDE

CONFIGURING SALES ORDER MANAGEMENT WITHIN DYNAMICS 365 FOR FINANCE & OPERATIONS
MODULE 1: CONFIGURING SALES ORDER MANAGEMENT CONTROLS

Opening the Customer Reasons maintenance form

How to do it...

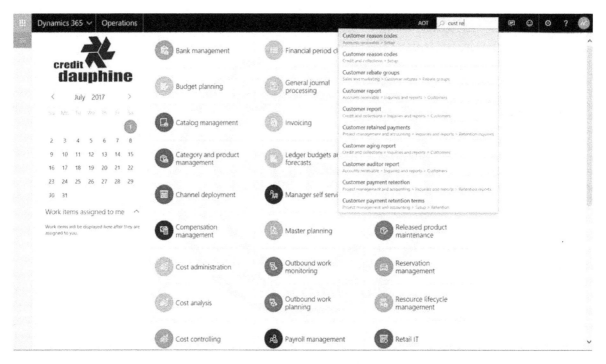

Step 2: Open the Customer reason codes form through the menu search

Another way that we can find the **Customer reason codes** form is through the menu search feature.

We can do this by clicking on the search icon in the header of the form (or by pressing **ALT+G**) and then type in **cust re** into the search box. Then you will be able to select the **Customer reason codes** form from the dropdown list.

dyn c
www.dynamicscompanions.com
Dynamics Companions

- 34 -

www.blindsquirrelpublishing.com
© 2019 Blind Squirrel Publishing, LLC , All Rights Reserved

BLIND SQUIRREL
PUBLISHING

DYNAMICS COMPANIONS
BARE BONES CONFIGURATION GUIDE

CONFIGURING SALES ORDER MANAGEMENT WITHIN DYNAMICS 365 FOR FINANCE & OPERATIONS
MODULE 1: CONFIGURING SALES ORDER MANAGEMENT CONTROLS

Opening the Customer Reasons maintenance form

How to do it...

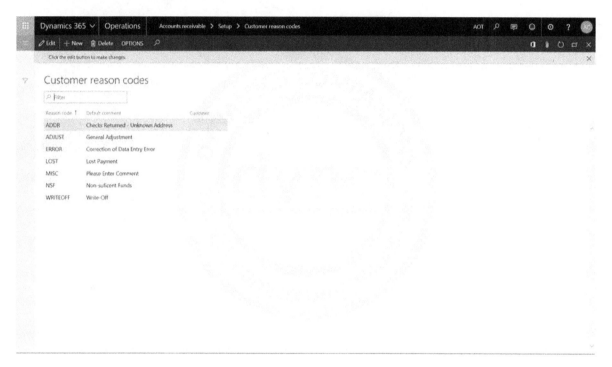

Step 2: Open the Customer reason codes form through the menu search

This will open up the Customer reason codes maintenance form where we can maintain our order reason codes.

dync

www.dynamicscompanions.com
Dynamics Companions

- 35 -

www.blindsquirrelpublishing.com
© 2019 Blind Squirrel Publishing, LLC , All Rights Reserved

BLIND SQUIRREL
PUBLISHING

DYNAMICS COMPANIONS
BARE BONES CONFIGURATION GUIDE

CONFIGURING SALES ORDER MANAGEMENT WITHIN DYNAMICS 365 FOR FINANCE & OPERATIONS
MODULE 1: CONFIGURING SALES ORDER MANAGEMENT CONTROLS

Opening the Customer Reasons maintenance form

How to do it...

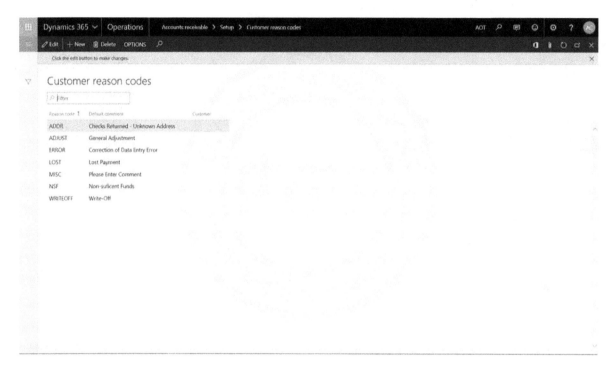

Step 2: Open the Customer reason codes form through the menu search

When the **Customer Reasons** maintenance form is displayed, you will notice that there are existing reason codes that have been entered in during the setup of the other modules.

You will notice that there are existing reason codes that have been entered in during the setup of the other modules. Now we can add some more for the Sales Order Processing.

dyn
www.dynamicscompanions.com
Dynamics Companions

- 36 -

www.blindsquirrelpublishing.com
© 2019 Blind Squirrel Publishing, LLC , All Rights Reserved

BLIND SQUIRREL
PUBLISHING

DYNAMICS COMPANIONS
BARE BONES CONFIGURATION GUIDE

CONFIGURING SALES ORDER MANAGEMENT WITHIN DYNAMICS 365 FOR FINANCE & OPERATIONS
MODULE 1: CONFIGURING SALES ORDER MANAGEMENT CONTROLS

Selecting Existing Reason Codes

As we pointed out before, there are a few reason codes already in the form that were created as we set up the other modules, and some of them are useful to be tracked within the Sales order processing module as well.

Rather than creating new records, we can mark them to be used within this module as well.

How to do it...

Step 1: Click on the Edit button

If the form is in read only mode, then we will want to switch it to edit mode so that we can make changes.

Click on the **Edit** button.

Now that we are in edit mode we

Step 2: Update the ERROR Customer, update the LOST Customer, update the MISC Customer and update the WRITEOFF

To do this we just need to select the reason codes that we want to reuse.

Set the ERROR Customer to Checked, change the LOST Customer to Checked, change the MISC Customer to Checked and set the WRITEOFF to Checked.

www.dynamicscompanions.com
Dynamics Companions

BLIND SQUIRREL
PUBLISHING

DYNAMICS COMPANIONS
BARE BONES CONFIGURATION GUIDE

CONFIGURING SALES ORDER MANAGEMENT WITHIN DYNAMICS 365 FOR FINANCE & OPERATIONS
MODULE 1: CONFIGURING SALES ORDER MANAGEMENT CONTROLS

Selecting Existing Reason Codes

How to do it...

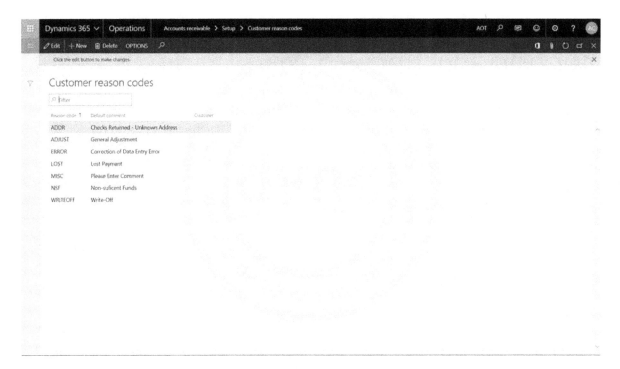

Step 1: Click on the Edit button

If the form is in read only mode, then we will want to switch it to edit mode so that we can make changes.

To do this just click on the **Edit** button in the menu bar.

www.dynamicscompanions.com
Dynamics Companions

- 38 -

www.blindsquirrelpublishing.com
© 2019 Blind Squirrel Publishing, LLC , All Rights Reserved

BLIND SQUIRREL
PUBLISHING

DYNAMICS COMPANIONS
BARE BONES CONFIGURATION GUIDE

CONFIGURING SALES ORDER MANAGEMENT WITHIN DYNAMICS 365 FOR FINANCE & OPERATIONS
MODULE 1: CONFIGURING SALES ORDER MANAGEMENT CONTROLS

Selecting Existing Reason Codes

How to do it...

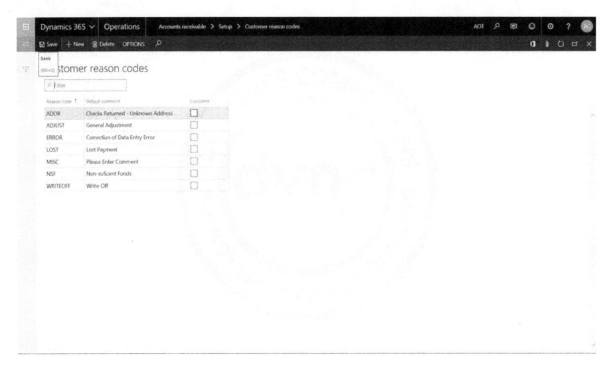

Step 1: Click on the Edit button

Now that we are in edit mode we

dyn c
www.dynamicscompanions.com
Dynamics Companions

- 39 -

www.blindsquirrelpublishing.com
© 2019 Blind Squirrel Publishing, LLC , All Rights Reserved

BLIND SQUIRREL
PUBLISHING

DYNAMICS COMPANIONS
BARE BONES CONFIGURATION GUIDE

CONFIGURING SALES ORDER MANAGEMENT WITHIN DYNAMICS 365 FOR FINANCE & OPERATIONS
MODULE 1: CONFIGURING SALES ORDER MANAGEMENT CONTROLS

Selecting Existing Reason Codes

How to do it...

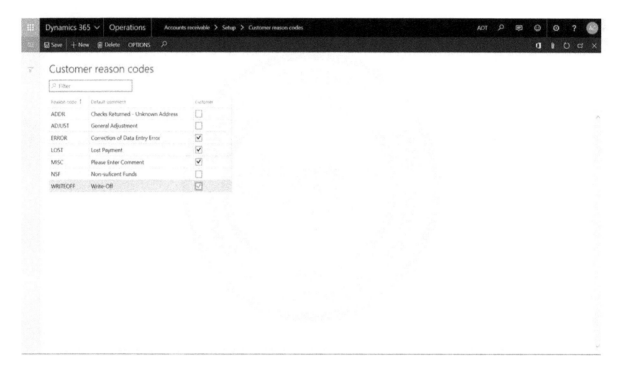

Step 2: Update the ERROR Customer, update the LOST Customer, update the MISC Customer and update the WRITEOFF

To do this we just need to select the reason codes that we want to reuse.

To do this we will just need to update the **ERROR Customer** value, change the **LOST Customer** value, change the **MISC Customer** value and update the **WRITEOFF** value.

For this example, we will want to set the **ERROR Customer** to **Checked**, set the **LOST Customer** to **Checked**, set the **MISC Customer** to **Checked** and set the **WRITEOFF** to **Checked**.

dyn c
www.dynamicscompanions.com
Dynamics Companions

- 40 -

www.blindsquirrelpublishing.com
© 2019 Blind Squirrel Publishing, LLC , All Rights Reserved

BLIND SQUIRREL
PUBLISHING

DYNAMICS COMPANIONS
BARE BONES CONFIGURATION GUIDE

CONFIGURING SALES ORDER MANAGEMENT WITHIN DYNAMICS 365 FOR FINANCE & OPERATIONS
MODULE 1: CONFIGURING SALES ORDER MANAGEMENT CONTROLS

Creating a Price Change Reason Code

Now we can start adding some additional reason codes that are specific to the Sales order processing area within the system.

Let's start off by creating a reason code that we can use whenever someone changes the price on a sales order to justify the change of the default price.

How to do it...

Step 1: Click on the New button

We will start off by creating a new record within the Customer reason code form.

Click on the **New** button.

Step 2: Update the Reason code

We will then give our reason code a code that we can reference it by.

Set the Reason code to PRICE.

Step 3: Update the Default comment

And then we will want to give the code a default comment that will show up in the reason dialog that the user could keep, or update.

Set the Default comment to Price Change.

www.dynamicscompanions.com
Dynamics Companions

- 41 -

www.blindsquirrelpublishing.com
© 2019 Blind Squirrel Publishing, LLC, All Rights Reserved

BLIND SQUIRREL
PUBLISHING

DYNAMICS COMPANIONS
BARE BONES CONFIGURATION GUIDE

CONFIGURING SALES ORDER MANAGEMENT WITHIN DYNAMICS 365 FOR FINANCE & OPERATIONS
MODULE 1: CONFIGURING SALES ORDER MANAGEMENT CONTROLS

Creating a Price Change Reason Code

How to do it...

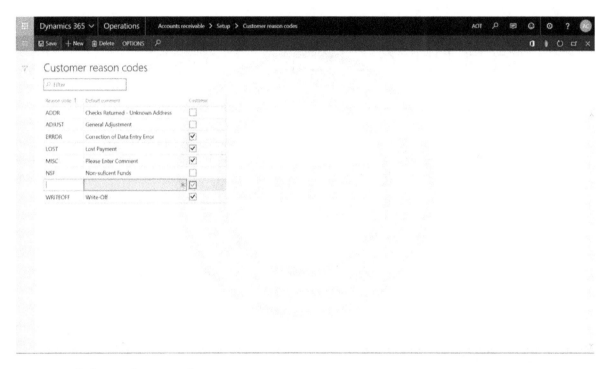

Step 1: Click on the New button

We will start off by creating a new record within the Customer reason code form.

To do this just click on the **New** button in the menu bar.

dyn c
www.dynamicscompanions.com
Dynamics Companions

- 42 -

www.blindsquirrelpublishing.com
© 2019 Blind Squirrel Publishing, LLC , All Rights Reserved

BLIND SQUIRREL
PUBLISHING

DYNAMICS COMPANIONS
BARE BONES CONFIGURATION GUIDE

CONFIGURING SALES ORDER MANAGEMENT WITHIN DYNAMICS 365 FOR FINANCE & OPERATIONS
MODULE 1: CONFIGURING SALES ORDER MANAGEMENT CONTROLS

Creating a Price Change Reason Code

How to do it...

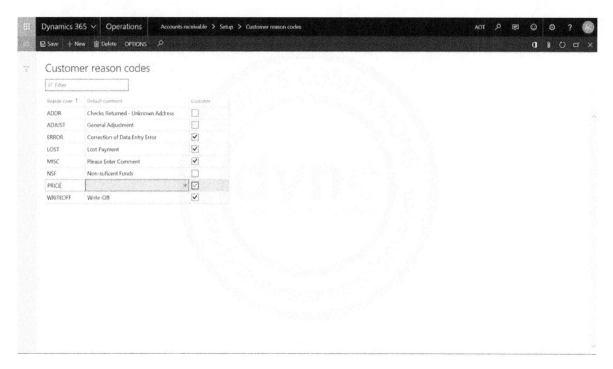

Step 2: Update the Reason code

We will then give our reason code a code that we can reference it by.

To do this just change the **Reason code** value.

For this example, we will want to set the **Reason code** to **PRICE**.

dync
www.dynamicscompanions.com
Dynamics Companions

- 43 -

www.blindsquirrelpublishing.com
© 2019 Blind Squirrel Publishing, LLC , All Rights Reserved

BLIND SQUIRREL
PUBLISHING

DYNAMICS COMPANIONS
BARE BONES CONFIGURATION GUIDE

CONFIGURING SALES ORDER MANAGEMENT WITHIN DYNAMICS 365 FOR FINANCE & OPERATIONS
MODULE 1: CONFIGURING SALES ORDER MANAGEMENT CONTROLS

Creating a Price Change Reason Code

How to do it...

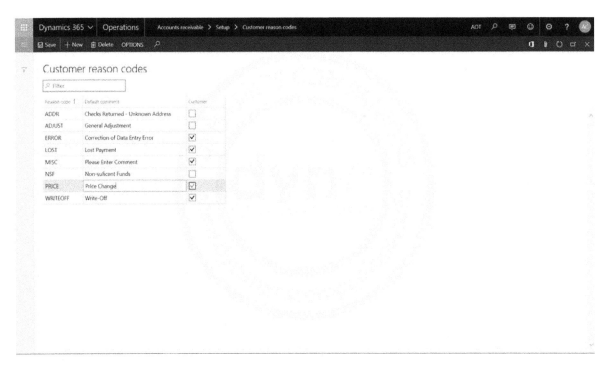

Step 3: Update the Default comment

And then we will want to give the code a default comment that will show up in the reason dialog that the user could keep, or update.

To do this we will just need to update the **Default comment** value.

For this example, we will want to set the **Default comment** to **Price Change**.

www.dynamicscompanions.com
Dynamics Companions

- 44 -

www.blindsquirrelpublishing.com
© 2019 Blind Squirrel Publishing, LLC , All Rights Reserved

BLIND SQUIRREL
PUBLISHING

DYNAMICS COMPANIONS
BARE BONES CONFIGURATION GUIDE

CONFIGURING SALES ORDER MANAGEMENT WITHIN DYNAMICS 365 FOR FINANCE & OPERATIONS
MODULE 1: CONFIGURING SALES ORDER MANAGEMENT CONTROLS

Creating a Quality Reason Code

Let's continue on and create another reason code.

This reason code would be for quality problems.

How to do it...

Step 1: Click on the New button

We will want to create a new record again within the Customer reason codes form.

Click on the **New** button.

Step 2: Update the Reason code

Now that we have a new record, we will want to give it a code that we can reference it by.

Set the Reason code to QUALITY.

Step 3: Update the Default comment

And next we will want to add a default comment that will be used when this reason code is used.

Set the Default comment to Quality issue.

dync
www.dynamicscompanions.com
Dynamics Companions

- 45 -

www.blindsquirrelpublishing.com
© 2019 Blind Squirrel Publishing, LLC , All Rights Reserved

BLIND SQUIRREL
PUBLISHING

DYNAMICS COMPANIONS
BARE BONES CONFIGURATION GUIDE

CONFIGURING SALES ORDER MANAGEMENT WITHIN DYNAMICS 365 FOR FINANCE & OPERATIONS
MODULE 1: CONFIGURING SALES ORDER MANAGEMENT CONTROLS

Creating a Quality Reason Code

How to do it...

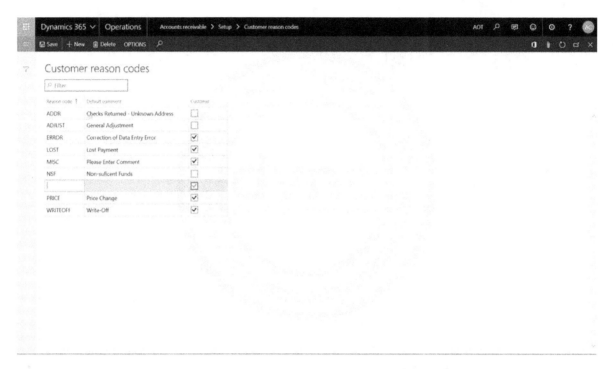

Step 1: Click on the New button

We will want to create a new record again within the Customer reason codes form.

To do this all we need to do is click on the **New** button in the menu bar.

www.dynamicscompanions.com
Dynamics Companions

- 46 -

www.blindsquirrelpublishing.com
© 2019 Blind Squirrel Publishing, LLC, All Rights Reserved

BLIND SQUIRREL
PUBLISHING

DYNAMICS COMPANIONS
BARE BONES CONFIGURATION GUIDE

CONFIGURING SALES ORDER MANAGEMENT WITHIN DYNAMICS 365 FOR FINANCE & OPERATIONS
MODULE 1: CONFIGURING SALES ORDER MANAGEMENT CONTROLS

Creating a Quality Reason Code

How to do it...

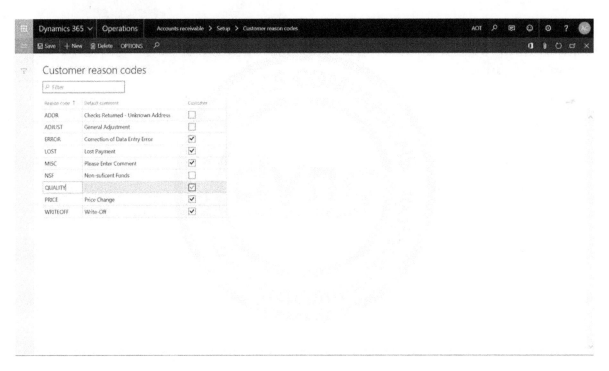

Step 2: Update the Reason code

Now that we have a new record, we will want to give it a code that we can reference it by.

To do this we will just need to change the **Reason code** value.

This time, we will want to set the **Reason code** to **QUALITY**.

dyn c
www.dynamicscompanions.com
Dynamics Companions

- 47 -

www.blindsquirrelpublishing.com
© 2019 Blind Squirrel Publishing, LLC , All Rights Reserved

BLIND SQUIRREL
PUBLISHING

DYNAMICS COMPANIONS
BARE BONES CONFIGURATION GUIDE

CONFIGURING SALES ORDER MANAGEMENT WITHIN DYNAMICS 365 FOR FINANCE & OPERATIONS
MODULE 1: CONFIGURING SALES ORDER MANAGEMENT CONTROLS

Creating a Quality Reason Code

How to do it...

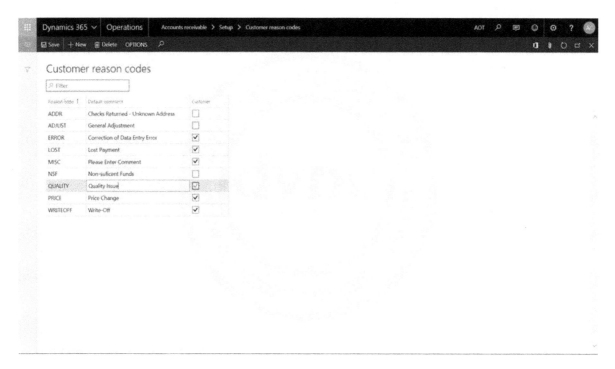

Step 3: Update the Default comment

And next we will want to add a default comment that will be used when this reason code is used.

To do this we will just need to update the **Default comment** value.

For this example, we will want to set the **Default comment** to **Quality issue**.

dyn c
www.dynamicscompanions.com
Dynamics Companions

- 48 -

www.blindsquirrelpublishing.com
© 2019 Blind Squirrel Publishing, LLC , All Rights Reserved

BLIND SQUIRREL
PUBLISHING

DYNAMICS COMPANIONS
BARE BONES CONFIGURATION GUIDE

CONFIGURING SALES ORDER MANAGEMENT WITHIN DYNAMICS 365 FOR FINANCE & OPERATIONS
MODULE 1: CONFIGURING SALES ORDER MANAGEMENT CONTROLS

Creating a Quality Reason Code

How to do it...

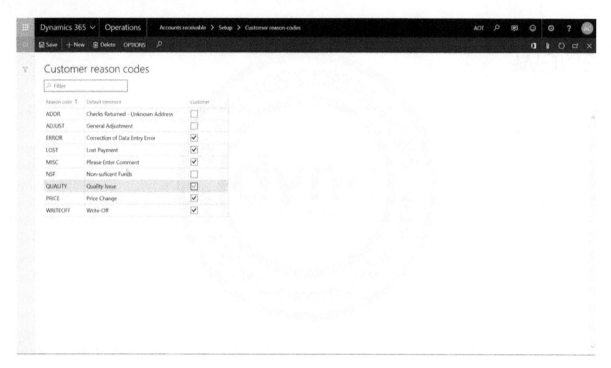

Step 3: Update the Default comment

After we have done that we are done and can exit from the form.

www.dynamicscompanions.com
Dynamics Companions

- 49 -

www.blindsquirrelpublishing.com
© 2019 Blind Squirrel Publishing, LLC , All Rights Reserved

BLIND SQUIRREL
PUBLISHING

DYNAMICS COMPANIONS
BARE BONES CONFIGURATION GUIIDE

CONFIGURING SALES ORDER MANAGEMENT WITHIN DYNAMICS 365 FOR FINANCE & OPERATIONS
MODULE 1: CONFIGURING SALES ORDER MANAGEMENT CONTROLS

Review

Now we have some auditing reason codes set up that we can use as we are processing the sales orders and tracking exceptions.

DYNAMICS COMPANIONS
BARE BONES CONFIGURATION GUIDE

CONFIGURING SALES ORDER MANAGEMENT WITHIN DYNAMICS 365 FOR FINANCE & OPERATIONS
MODULE 1: CONFIGURING SALES ORDER MANAGEMENT CONTROLS

Configuring Delivery Terms

Next we will configure a few **Delivery Terms** codes that we will be able to use within our Sales Orders.

Topics Covered

- Opening up the Terms of delivery maintenance form

- Setting up a Cost and Freight Delivery Terms code

- Adding a Cost, Insurance & Freight Delivery Terms Code

- Adding a Carriage Paid to Delivery Terms Code

- Adding a Delivered at Frontier Delivery Terms Code

- Adding a Delivery Duty Paid Delivery Terms Code

- Adding a Delivery Excluding Shipping Terms of Delivery code

- Adding an Ex-Works shipping Terms of Delivery code

- Adding a Free Alongside Ship Terms of Delivery code

- Adding a Free Carrier Terms of Delivery code

- Adding a Free On Board Terms of Delivery Code

- Summary

 www.dynamicscompanions.com
Dynamics Companions

- 51 -

www.blindsquirrelpublishing.com
© 2019 Blind Squirrel Publishing, LLC , All Rights Reserved

BLIND SQUIRREL
PUBLISHING

DYNAMICS COMPANIONS
BARE BONES CONFIGURATION GUIDE

CONFIGURING SALES ORDER MANAGEMENT WITHIN DYNAMICS 365 FOR FINANCE & OPERATIONS
MODULE 1: CONFIGURING SALES ORDER MANAGEMENT CONTROLS

Opening up the Terms of delivery maintenance form

We will need to open up the maintenance form that we used to maintain the **Terms of delivery** codes within the system.

How to do it...

Step 1: Open the Terms of Delivery form through the menu

We can get to the **Terms of Delivery** form a couple of different ways. The first way is through the master menu.

Navigate to Sales and Marketing > Setup > Distribution > Terms of Delivery.

Step 2: Open the Terms of delivery form through the menu search

Another way that we can find the **Terms of delivery** form is through the menu search feature.

Type in **terms of deliv** into the menu search and select **Terms of delivery**.

This will open up the **Terms of delivery** maintenance form for us.

If you have set up the Procurement and Sourcing module then you my notice that there are already a number of standard delivery terms codes that are in this form. That is because they are shared between the modules.

DYNAMICS COMPANIONS
BARE BONES CONFIGURATION GUIDE

CONFIGURING SALES ORDER MANAGEMENT WITHIN DYNAMICS 365 FOR FINANCE & OPERATIONS
MODULE 1: CONFIGURING SALES ORDER MANAGEMENT CONTROLS

Opening up the Terms of delivery maintenance form

How to do it...

Step 1: Open the Terms of Delivery form through the menu

We can get to the **Terms of Delivery** form a couple of different ways. The first way is through the master menu.

In order to do this, open up the navigation panel, expand out the **Modules** and group, and click on **Sales and Marketing** to see all of the menu items that are available. Then click on the **Terms of Delivery** menu item within the **Distribution** folder of the **Setup** group.

dyn c
www.dynamicscompanions.com
Dynamics Companions

- 53 -

www.blindsquirrelpublishing.com
© 2019 Blind Squirrel Publishing, LLC , All Rights Reserved

BLIND SQUIRREL
PUBLISHING

DYNAMICS COMPANIONS
BARE BONES CONFIGURATION GUIDE

CONFIGURING SALES ORDER MANAGEMENT WITHIN DYNAMICS 365 FOR FINANCE & OPERATIONS
MODULE 1: CONFIGURING SALES ORDER MANAGEMENT CONTROLS

Opening up the Terms of delivery maintenance form

How to do it...

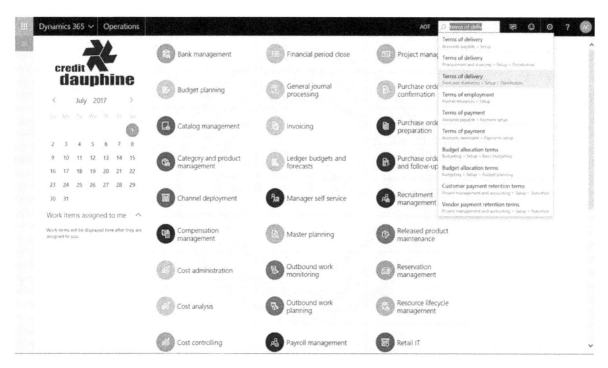

Step 2: Open the Terms of delivery form through the menu search

Another way that we can find the **Terms of delivery** form is through the menu search feature.

We can do this by clicking on the search icon in the header of the form (or by pressing **ALT+G**) and then type in **terms of deliv** into the search box. Then you will be able to select the **Terms of delivery** form from the dropdown list.

DYNAMICS COMPANIONS
BARE BONES CONFIGURATION GUIDE

CONFIGURING SALES ORDER MANAGEMENT WITHIN DYNAMICS 365 FOR FINANCE & OPERATIONS
MODULE 1: CONFIGURING SALES ORDER MANAGEMENT CONTROLS

Opening up the Terms of delivery maintenance form

How to do it...

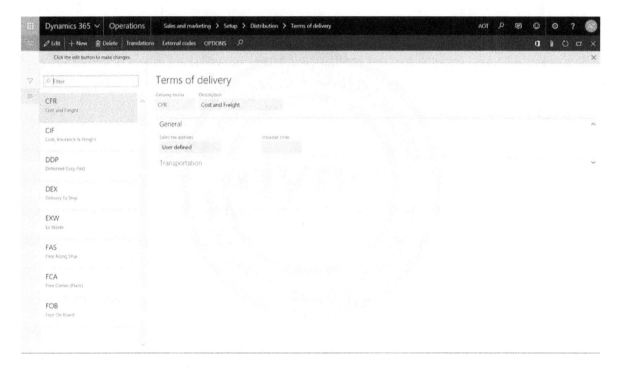

Step 2: Open the Terms of delivery form through the menu search

This will open up the **Terms of delivery** maintenance form for us.

If you have set up the Procurement and Sourcing module then you my notice that there are already a number of standard delivery terms codes that are in this form. That is because they are shared between the modules.

www.dynamicscompanions.com
Dynamics Companions

- 55 -

www.blindsquirrelpublishing.com
© 2019 Blind Squirrel Publishing, LLC , All Rights Reserved

BLIND SQUIRREL
PUBLISHING

DYNAMICS COMPANIONS
BARE BONES CONFIGURATION GUIDE

CONFIGURING SALES ORDER MANAGEMENT WITHIN DYNAMICS 365 FOR FINANCE & OPERATIONS
MODULE 1: CONFIGURING SALES ORDER MANAGEMENT CONTROLS

Setting up a Cost and Freight Delivery Terms code

If you don't have any terms of delivery codes configured yet, then we will need to add them to the system.

We will start off by setting up our first delivery terms code code.

How to do it...

Step 1: Click New

We will start off by creating a new Terms of delivery record.

Click on the **New** button.

Step 2: Update the Delivery terms

We will now want to give our new record a delivery terms code that we can reference it by.

Set the Delivery terms to CFR.

Step 3: Update the Description

And then we will want to give our new terms of delivery record a more detailed description.

Set the Description to Cost and freight.

 www.dynamicscompanions.com
Dynamics Companions

- 56 -

www.blindsquirrelpublishing.com
© 2019 Blind Squirrel Publishing, LLC , All Rights Reserved

 BLIND SQUIRREL
PUBLISHING

DYNAMICS COMPANIONS
BARE BONES CONFIGURATION GUIDE

CONFIGURING SALES ORDER MANAGEMENT WITHIN DYNAMICS 365 FOR FINANCE & OPERATIONS
MODULE 1: CONFIGURING SALES ORDER MANAGEMENT CONTROLS

Setting up a Cost and Freight Delivery Terms code

How to do it...

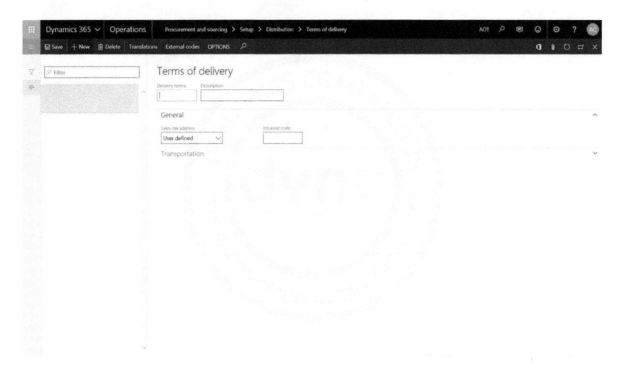

Step 1: Click New

We will start off by creating a new Terms of delivery record.

To do this just click on the **New** button.

DYNAMICS COMPANIONS
BARE BONES CONFIGURATION GUIDE

CONFIGURING SALES ORDER MANAGEMENT WITHIN DYNAMICS 365 FOR FINANCE & OPERATIONS
MODULE 1: CONFIGURING SALES ORDER MANAGEMENT CONTROLS

Setting up a Cost and Freight Delivery Terms code

How to do it...

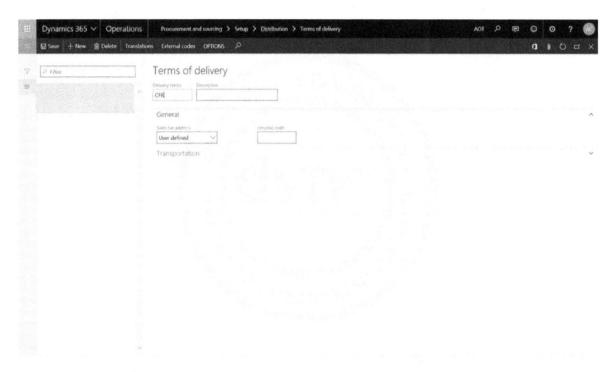

Step 2: Update the Delivery terms

We will now want to give our new record a delivery terms code that we can reference it by.

To do this we will just need to update the **Delivery terms** value.

For this example, we will want to set the **Delivery terms** to **CFR**.

www.dynamicscompanions.com
Dynamics Companions

- 58 -

www.blindsquirrelpublishing.com
© 2019 Blind Squirrel Publishing, LLC, All Rights Reserved

BLIND SQUIRREL
PUBLISHING

DYNAMICS COMPANIONS
BARE BONES CONFIGURATION GUIDE

CONFIGURING SALES ORDER MANAGEMENT WITHIN DYNAMICS 365 FOR FINANCE & OPERATIONS
MODULE 1: CONFIGURING SALES ORDER MANAGEMENT CONTROLS

Setting up a Cost and Freight Delivery Terms code

How to do it...

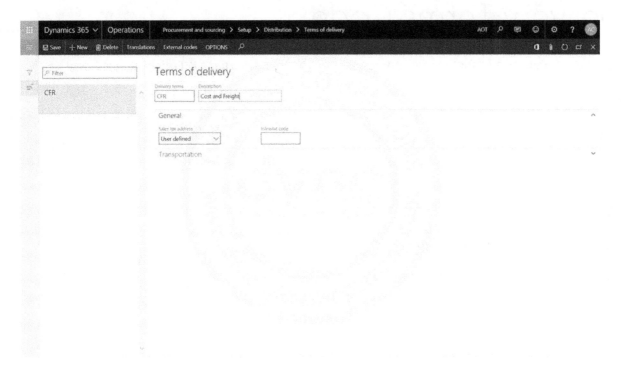

Step 3: Update the Description

And then we will want to give our new terms of delivery record a more detailed description.

To do this we will just need to update the **Description** value.

For this example, we will want to set the **Description** to **Cost and freight**.

dyn c

www.dynamicscompanions.com
Dynamics Companions

- 59 -

www.blindsquirrelpublishing.com
© 2019 Blind Squirrel Publishing, LLC , All Rights Reserved

BLIND SQUIRREL
PUBLISHING

DYNAMICS COMPANIONS
BARE BONES CONFIGURATION GUIDE

CONFIGURING SALES ORDER MANAGEMENT WITHIN DYNAMICS 365 FOR FINANCE & OPERATIONS
MODULE 1: CONFIGURING SALES ORDER MANAGEMENT CONTROLS

Adding a Cost, Insurance & Freight Delivery Terms Code

Next we will want to add another delivery terms code for **Cost, Insurance & Freight**.

How to do it...

Step 1: Click New

To do this we will add another terms of delivery record.

Click on the **New** button.

Step 2: Update the Delivery Terms

We will now want to give our delivery terms record a code to reference it.

Set the Delivery Terms to CIF.

Step 3: Update the Description

Then we will want to give our new record a more detailed description to describe the delivery terms code.

Set the Description to Cost Insurance & Freight.

 www.dynamicscompanions.com
Dynamics Companions

- 60 -

www.blindsquirrelpublishing.com
© 2019 Blind Squirrel Publishing, LLC , All Rights Reserved

BLIND SQUIRREL
PUBLISHING

DYNAMICS COMPANIONS
BARE BONES CONFIGURATION GUIDE

CONFIGURING SALES ORDER MANAGEMENT WITHIN DYNAMICS 365 FOR FINANCE & OPERATIONS
MODULE 1: CONFIGURING SALES ORDER MANAGEMENT CONTROLS

Adding a Cost, Insurance & Freight Delivery Terms Code

How to do it...

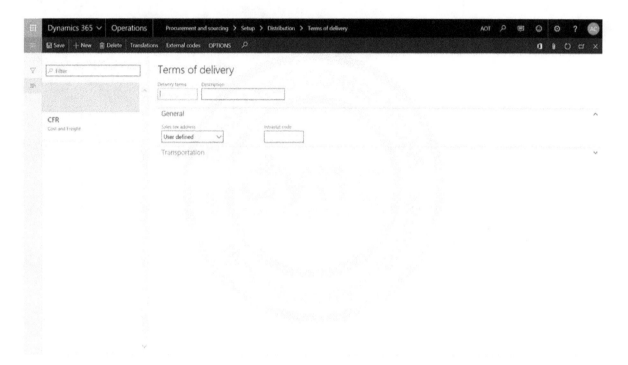

Step 1: Click New

To do this we will add another terms of delivery record.

To do this just click on the **New** button.

dyn©
Dynamics Companions
www.dynamicscompanions.com

- 61 -

www.blindsquirrelpublishing.com
© 2019 Blind Squirrel Publishing, LLC, All Rights Reserved

BLIND SQUIRREL
PUBLISHING

DYNAMICS COMPANIONS
BARE BONES CONFIGURATION GUIDE

CONFIGURING SALES ORDER MANAGEMENT WITHIN DYNAMICS 365 FOR FINANCE & OPERATIONS
MODULE 1: CONFIGURING SALES ORDER MANAGEMENT CONTROLS

Adding a Cost, Insurance & Freight Delivery Terms Code

How to do it...

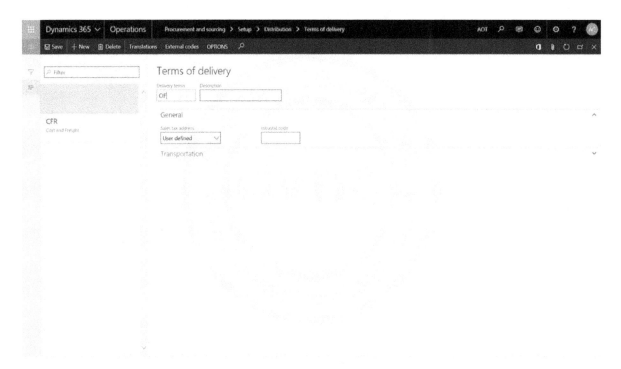

Step 2: Update the Delivery Terms

We will now want to give our delivery terms record a code to reference it.

To do this we will just need to update the **Delivery Terms** value.

For this example, we will want to set the **Delivery Terms** to **CIF**.

dyn c
www.dynamicscompanions.com
Dynamics Companions

- 62 -

www.blindsquirrelpublishing.com
© 2019 Blind Squirrel Publishing, LLC , All Rights Reserved

BLIND SQUIRREL
PUBLISHING

DYNAMICS COMPANIONS
BARE BONES CONFIGURATION GUIDE

CONFIGURING SALES ORDER MANAGEMENT WITHIN DYNAMICS 365 FOR FINANCE & OPERATIONS
MODULE 1: CONFIGURING SALES ORDER MANAGEMENT CONTROLS

Adding a Cost, Insurance & Freight Delivery Terms Code

How to do it...

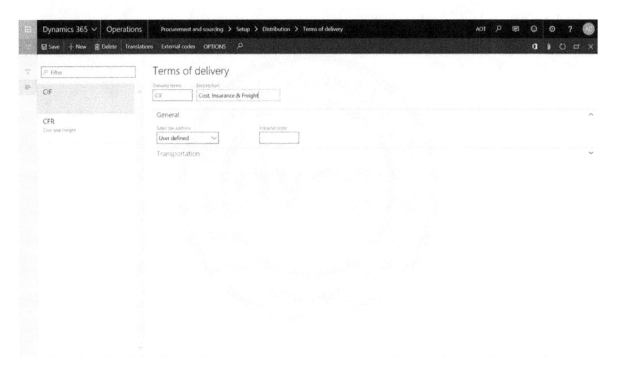

Step 3: Update the Description

Then we will want to give our new record a more detailed description to describe the delivery terms code.

To do this we will just need to update the **Description** value.

For this example, we will want to set the **Description** to **Cost Insurance & Freight**.

dync
www.dynamicscompanions.com
Dynamics Companions
- 63 -
www.blindsquirrelpublishing.com
© 2019 Blind Squirrel Publishing, LLC , All Rights Reserved
BLIND SQUIRREL
PUBLISHING

DYNAMICS COMPANIONS
BARE BONES CONFIGURATION GUIDE

CONFIGURING SALES ORDER MANAGEMENT WITHIN DYNAMICS 365 FOR FINANCE & OPERATIONS
MODULE 1: CONFIGURING SALES ORDER MANAGEMENT CONTROLS

Adding a Carriage Paid to Delivery Terms Code

Now we will add another delivery terms code for Delivery Duty Paid.

DYNAMICS COMPANIONS
BARE BONES CONFIGURATION GUIDE

CONFIGURING SALES ORDER MANAGEMENT WITHIN DYNAMICS 365 FOR FINANCE & OPERATIONS
MODULE 1: CONFIGURING SALES ORDER MANAGEMENT CONTROLS

Adding a Delivered at Frontier Delivery Terms Code

Now we will add another delivery terms code for Delivery Duty Paid.

DYNAMICS COMPANIONS
BARE BONES CONFIGURATION GUIDE

CONFIGURING SALES ORDER MANAGEMENT WITHIN DYNAMICS 365 FOR FINANCE & OPERATIONS
MODULE 1: CONFIGURING SALES ORDER MANAGEMENT CONTROLS

Adding a Delivery Duty Paid Delivery Terms Code

Now we will add another delivery terms code for Delivery Duty Paid.

How to do it...

Step 1: Click New

We will want to create a new **Terms of delivery** record.

Click on the **New** button.

Step 2: Update the Delivery terms

Next we will want to give our Terms of delivery record a **Delivery terms** code.

Set the Delivery terms to DDF.

Step 3: Update the Description

And then we will want to give our terms of delivery a more detailed description.

Set the Description to Delivery Duty Paid.

DYNAMICS COMPANIONS
BARE BONES CONFIGURATION GUIDE

CONFIGURING SALES ORDER MANAGEMENT WITHIN DYNAMICS 365 FOR FINANCE & OPERATIONS
MODULE 1: CONFIGURING SALES ORDER MANAGEMENT CONTROLS

Adding a Delivery Duty Paid Delivery Terms Code

How to do it...

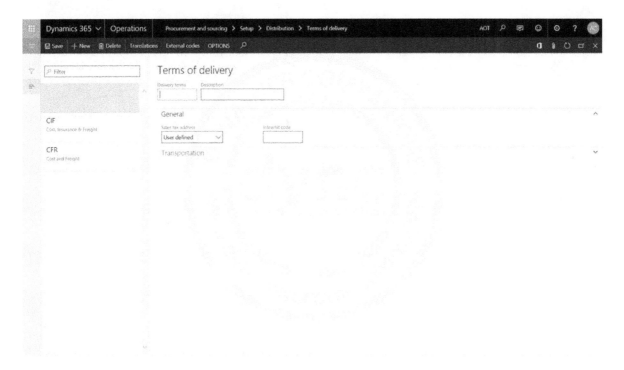

Step 1: Click New

We will want to create a new **Terms of delivery** record.

To do this just click on the **New** button.

dyn c
www.dynamicscompanions.com
Dynamics Companions

- 67 -

www.blindsquirrelpublishing.com
© 2019 Blind Squirrel Publishing, LLC, All Rights Reserved

BLIND SQUIRREL
PUBLISHING

DYNAMICS COMPANIONS
BARE BONES CONFIGURATION GUIDE

CONFIGURING SALES ORDER MANAGEMENT WITHIN DYNAMICS 365 FOR FINANCE & OPERATIONS
MODULE 1: CONFIGURING SALES ORDER MANAGEMENT CONTROLS

Adding a Delivery Duty Paid Delivery Terms Code

How to do it...

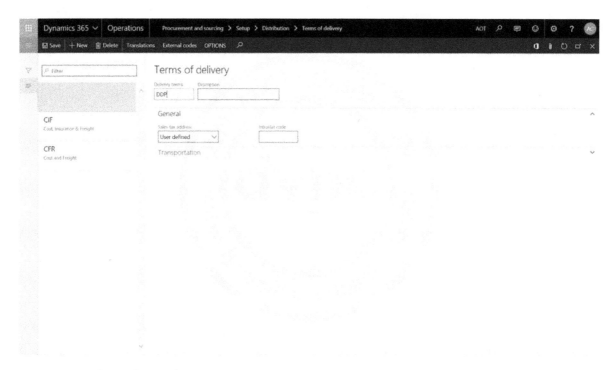

Step 2: Update the Delivery terms

Next we will want to give our Terms of delivery record a **Delivery terms** code.

To do this we will just need to update the **Delivery terms** value.

For this example, we will want to set the **Delivery terms** to **DDF**.

dyn c
www.dynamicscompanions.com
Dynamics Companions

- 68 -

www.blindsquirrelpublishing.com
© 2019 Blind Squirrel Publishing, LLC , All Rights Reserved

BLIND SQUIRREL
PUBLISHING

DYNAMICS COMPANIONS
BARE BONES CONFIGURATION GUIDE

CONFIGURING SALES ORDER MANAGEMENT WITHIN DYNAMICS 365 FOR FINANCE & OPERATIONS
MODULE 1: CONFIGURING SALES ORDER MANAGEMENT CONTROLS

Adding a Delivery Duty Paid Delivery Terms Code

How to do it...

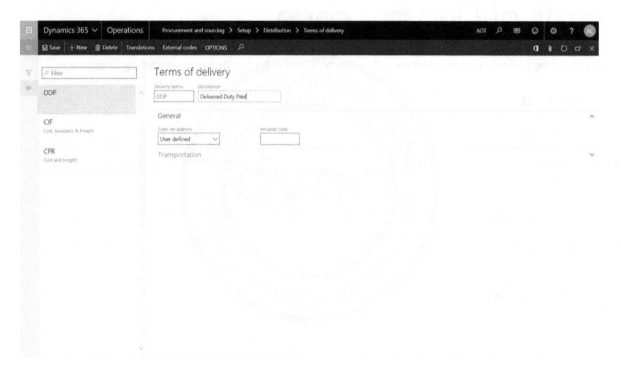

Step 3: Update the Description

And then we will want to give our terms of delivery a more detailed description.

To do this we will just need to update the **Description** value.

For this example, we will want to set the **Description** to **Delivery Duty Paid**.

dyn c
www.dynamicscompanions.com
Dynamics Companions

- 69 -

www.blindsquirrelpublishing.com
© 2019 Blind Squirrel Publishing, LLC, All Rights Reserved

BLIND SQUIRREL
PUBLISHING

DYNAMICS COMPANIONS
BARE BONES CONFIGURATION GUIDE

CONFIGURING SALES ORDER MANAGEMENT WITHIN DYNAMICS 365 FOR FINANCE & OPERATIONS
MODULE 1: CONFIGURING SALES ORDER MANAGEMENT CONTROLS

Adding a Delivery Excluding Shipping Terms of Delivery code

The next Terms of delivery code that we will want to add will be for **Delivery excluding shipping**.

How to do it...

Step 1: Click New

We will start off by creating a new **Terms of delivery** record.

Click on the **New** button.

Step 2: Update the Delivery terms

Now we will give our new Terms of delivery record a **Delivery terms** code.

Set the Delivery terms to DEX.

Step 3: Update the Description

And then we will want to give our Terms of delivery record a more detailed description.

Set the Description to Delivery Ex Ship.

dyn c
www.dynamicscompanions.com
Dynamics Companions

- 70 -

www.blindsquirrelpublishing.com
© 2019 Blind Squirrel Publishing, LLC , All Rights Reserved

BLIND SQUIRREL
PUBLISHING

DYNAMICS COMPANIONS
BARE BONES CONFIGURATION GUIDE

CONFIGURING SALES ORDER MANAGEMENT WITHIN DYNAMICS 365 FOR FINANCE & OPERATIONS
MODULE 1: CONFIGURING SALES ORDER MANAGEMENT CONTROLS

Adding a Delivery Excluding Shipping Terms of Delivery code

How to do it...

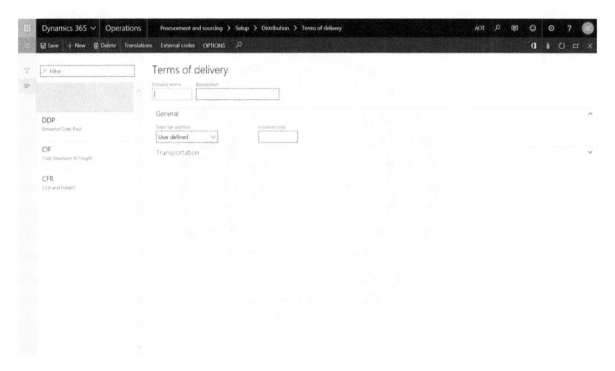

Step 1: Click New

We will start off by creating a new **Terms of delivery** record.

To do this just click on the **New** button.

www.dynamicscompanions.com
Dynamics Companions

- 71 -

www.blindsquirrelpublishing.com
© 2019 Blind Squirrel Publishing, LLC, All Rights Reserved

BLIND SQUIRREL
PUBLISHING

DYNAMICS COMPANIONS
BARE BONES CONFIGURATION GUIDE

CONFIGURING SALES ORDER MANAGEMENT WITHIN DYNAMICS 365 FOR FINANCE & OPERATIONS
MODULE 1: CONFIGURING SALES ORDER MANAGEMENT CONTROLS

Adding a Delivery Excluding Shipping Terms of Delivery code

How to do it...

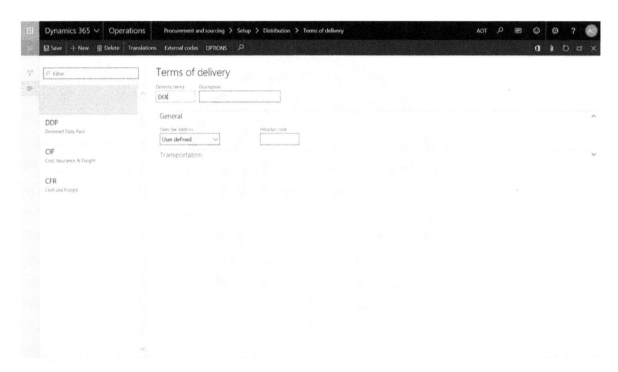

Step 2: Update the Delivery terms

Now we will give our new Terms of delivery record a **Delivery terms** code.

To do this we will just need to update the **Delivery terms** value.

For this example, we will want to set the **Delivery terms** to **DEX**.

www.dynamicscompanions.com
Dynamics Companions

www.blindsquirrelpublishing.com
© 2019 Blind Squirrel Publishing, LLC , All Rights Reserved

BLIND SQUIRREL
PUBLISHING

DYNAMICS COMPANIONS
BARE BONES CONFIGURATION GUIDE

CONFIGURING SALES ORDER MANAGEMENT WITHIN DYNAMICS 365 FOR FINANCE & OPERATIONS
MODULE 1: CONFIGURING SALES ORDER MANAGEMENT CONTROLS

Adding a Delivery Excluding Shipping Terms of Delivery code

How to do it...

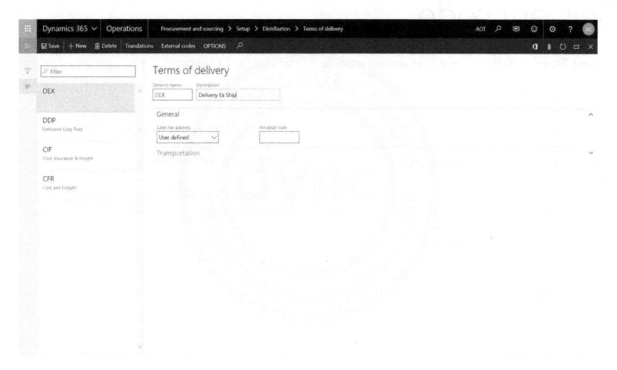

Step 3: Update the Description

And then we will want to give our Terms of delivery record a more detailed description.

To do this we will just need to update the **Description** value.

For this example, we will want to set the **Description** to **Delivery Ex Ship**.

dyn c
www.dynamicscompanions.com
Dynamics Companions

- 73 -

www.blindsquirrelpublishing.com
© 2019 Blind Squirrel Publishing, LLC, All Rights Reserved

BLIND SQUIRREL
PUBLISHING

DYNAMICS COMPANIONS
BARE BONES CONFIGURATION GUIDE

CONFIGURING SALES ORDER MANAGEMENT WITHIN DYNAMICS 365 FOR FINANCE & OPERATIONS
MODULE 1: CONFIGURING SALES ORDER MANAGEMENT CONTROLS

Adding an Ex-Works shipping Terms of Delivery code

The next Terms of delivery code that we will want to add will be for **Ex-works**.

How to do it...

Step 1: Click New

We will create another Terms of Delivery record.

Click on the **New** button.

Step 2: Update the Delivery terms

We will then want to give our new Terms of delivery record a **Delivery terms** code that we can reference it by.

Set the Delivery terms to EXW.

Step 3: Update the Description

And then we will want to give our Terms of delivery record amore detailed description for the users.

Set the Description to Ex Works.

dyn☐

www.dynamicscompanions.com
Dynamics Companions

- 74 -

www.blindsquirrelpublishing.com
© 2019 Blind Squirrel Publishing, LLC , All Rights Reserved

BLIND SQUIRREL
PUBLISHING

DYNAMICS COMPANIONS
BARE BONES CONFIGURATION GUIDE

CONFIGURING SALES ORDER MANAGEMENT WITHIN DYNAMICS 365 FOR FINANCE & OPERATIONS
MODULE 1: CONFIGURING SALES ORDER MANAGEMENT CONTROLS

Adding an Ex-Works shipping Terms of Delivery code

How to do it...

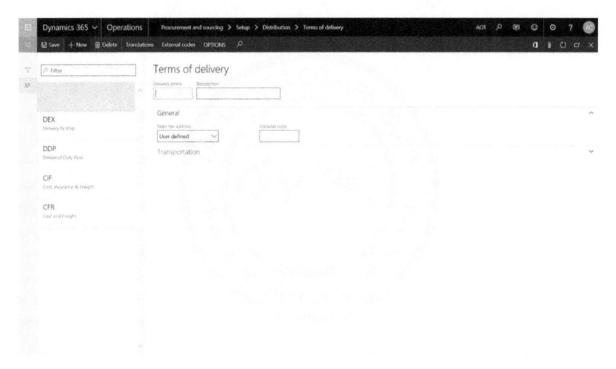

Step 1: Click New

We will create another Terms of Delivery record.

To do this just click on the **New** button.

www.dynamicscompanions.com
Dynamics Companions

- 75 -

www.blindsquirrelpublishing.com
© 2019 Blind Squirrel Publishing, LLC , All Rights Reserved

BLIND SQUIRREL
PUBLISHING

DYNAMICS COMPANIONS
BARE BONES CONFIGURATION GUIDE

CONFIGURING SALES ORDER MANAGEMENT WITHIN DYNAMICS 365 FOR FINANCE & OPERATIONS
MODULE 1: CONFIGURING SALES ORDER MANAGEMENT CONTROLS

Adding an Ex-Works shipping Terms of Delivery code

How to do it...

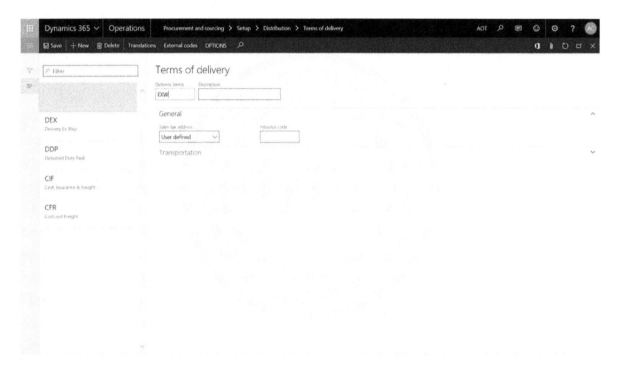

Step 2: Update the Delivery terms

We will then want to give our new Terms of delivery record a **Delivery terms** code that we can reference it by.

To do this we will just need to update the **Delivery terms** value.

For this example, we will want to set the **Delivery terms** to **EXW**.

www.dynamicscompanions.com
Dynamics Companions

- 76 -

www.blindsquirrelpublishing.com
© 2019 Blind Squirrel Publishing, LLC , All Rights Reserved

BLIND SQUIRREL
PUBLISHING

DYNAMICS COMPANIONS
BARE BONES CONFIGURATION GUIDE

CONFIGURING SALES ORDER MANAGEMENT WITHIN DYNAMICS 365 FOR FINANCE & OPERATIONS
MODULE 1: CONFIGURING SALES ORDER MANAGEMENT CONTROLS

Adding an Ex-Works shipping Terms of Delivery code

How to do it...

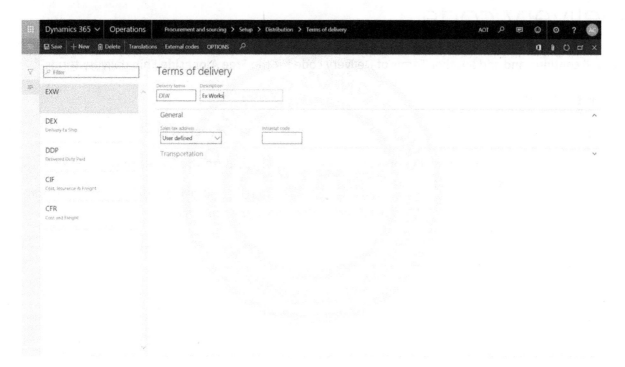

Step 3: Update the Description

And then we will want to give our Terms of delivery record amore detailed description for the users.

To do this we will just need to update the **Description** value.

For this example, we will want to set the **Description** to **Ex Works**.

www.dynamicscompanions.com
Dynamics Companions

- 77 -

www.blindsquirrelpublishing.com
© 2019 Blind Squirrel Publishing, LLC , All Rights Reserved

BLIND SQUIRREL
PUBLISHING

dync

DYNAMICS COMPANIONS
BARE BONES CONFIGURATION GUIDE

CONFIGURING SALES ORDER MANAGEMENT WITHIN DYNAMICS 365 FOR FINANCE & OPERATIONS
MODULE 1: CONFIGURING SALES ORDER MANAGEMENT CONTROLS

Adding a Free Alongside Ship Terms of Delivery code

We will continue and add another Terms of Delivery code for the **Free Alongside Ship** delivery terms.

How to do it...

Step 1: Click New

Just like the other terms of delivery records, we will start off by adding a new record within the **Terms of delivery** maintenance form.

Click on the **New** button.

Step 2: Update the Delivery terms

We will then give our new record a **Delivery terms** code to reference it by.

Set the Delivery terms to FAS.

Step 3: Update the Description

And then we will give our delivery terms a more detailed description.

Set the Description to Free Along Ship.

dyn c
www.dynamicscompanions.com
Dynamics Companions

- 78 -

www.blindsquirrelpublishing.com
© 2019 Blind Squirrel Publishing, LLC , All Rights Reserved

BLIND SQUIRREL
PUBLISHING

DYNAMICS COMPANIONS
BARE BONES CONFIGURATION GUIDE

CONFIGURING SALES ORDER MANAGEMENT WITHIN DYNAMICS 365 FOR FINANCE & OPERATIONS
MODULE 1: CONFIGURING SALES ORDER MANAGEMENT CONTROLS

Adding a Free Alongside Ship Terms of Delivery code

How to do it...

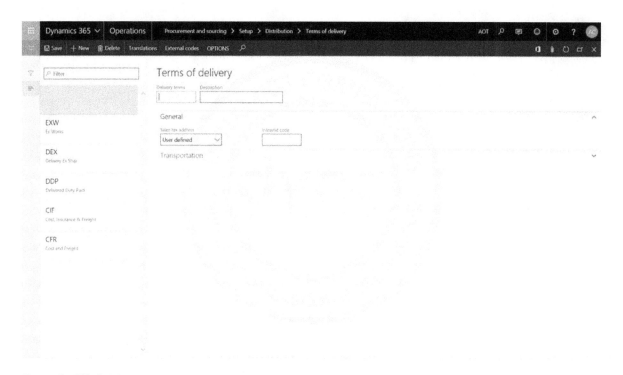

Step 1: Click New

Just like the other terms of delivery records, we will start off by adding a new record within the **Terms of delivery** maintenance form.

To do this just click on the **New** button.

www.dynamicscompanions.com
Dynamics Companions

- 79 -

www.blindsquirrelpublishing.com
© 2019 Blind Squirrel Publishing, LLC , All Rights Reserved

BLIND SQUIRREL
PUBLISHING

DYNAMICS COMPANIONS
BARE BONES CONFIGURATION GUIDE

CONFIGURING SALES ORDER MANAGEMENT WITHIN DYNAMICS 365 FOR FINANCE & OPERATIONS
MODULE 1: CONFIGURING SALES ORDER MANAGEMENT CONTROLS

Adding a Free Alongside Ship Terms of Delivery code

How to do it...

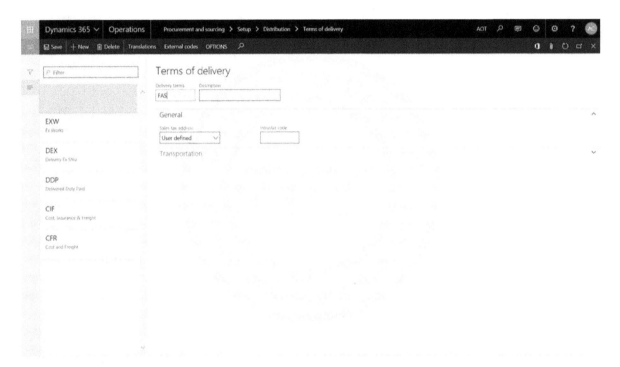

Step 2: Update the Delivery terms

We will then give our new record a **Delivery terms** code to reference it by.

To do this we will just need to update the **Delivery terms** value.

For this example, we will want to set the **Delivery terms** to **FAS**.

www.dynamicscompanions.com
Dynamics Companions

- 80 -

www.blindsquirrelpublishing.com
© 2019 Blind Squirrel Publishing, LLC , All Rights Reserved

BLIND SQUIRREL
PUBLISHING

DYNAMICS COMPANIONS
BARE BONES CONFIGURATION GUIDE

CONFIGURING SALES ORDER MANAGEMENT WITHIN DYNAMICS 365 FOR FINANCE & OPERATIONS
MODULE 1: CONFIGURING SALES ORDER MANAGEMENT CONTROLS

Adding a Free Alongside Ship Terms of Delivery code

How to do it...

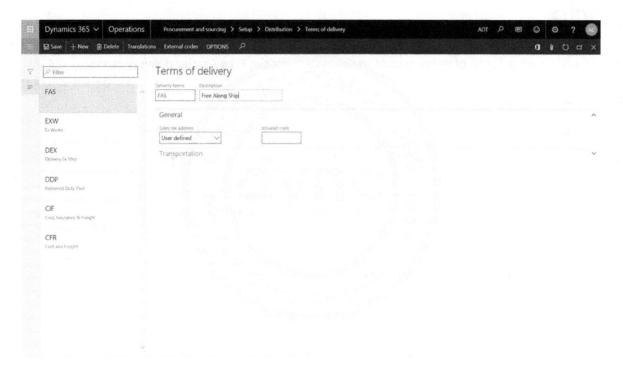

Step 3: Update the Description

And then we will give our delivery terms a more detailed description.

To do this we will just need to update the **Description** value.

For this example, we will want to set the **Description** to **Free Along Ship**.

dyn c
www.dynamicscompanions.com
Dynamics Companions

- 81 -

www.blindsquirrelpublishing.com
© 2019 Blind Squirrel Publishing, LLC, All Rights Reserved

BLIND SQUIRREL
PUBLISHING

DYNAMICS COMPANIONS
BARE BONES CONFIGURATION GUIDE

CONFIGURING SALES ORDER MANAGEMENT WITHIN DYNAMICS 365 FOR FINANCE & OPERATIONS
MODULE 1: CONFIGURING SALES ORDER MANAGEMENT CONTROLS

Adding a Free Carrier Terms of Delivery code

We will add another Terms of delivery code to the system for the **Free Carrier** delivery terms.

How to do it...

Step 1: Click New

We will insert another record into the **Terms of delivery** maintenance form.

Click on the **New** button.

Step 2: Update the Delivery terms

We will then give our new record a **Delivery terms** code.

Set the Delivery terms to FCA.

Step 3: Update the Description

And then we will give our Terms of delivery record a more detailed description so that the users can decipher the code.

Set the Description to Free Carrier (Place).

DYNAMICS COMPANIONS
BARE BONES CONFIGURATION GUIDE

CONFIGURING SALES ORDER MANAGEMENT WITHIN DYNAMICS 365 FOR FINANCE & OPERATIONS
MODULE 1: CONFIGURING SALES ORDER MANAGEMENT CONTROLS

Adding a Free Carrier Terms of Delivery code

How to do it...

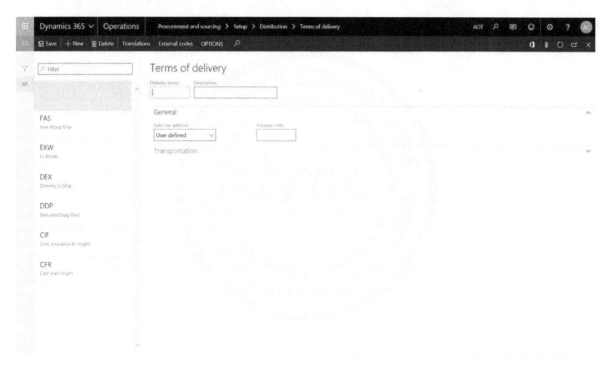

Step 1: Click New

We will insert another record into the **Terms of delivery** maintenance form.

To do this just click on the **New** button.

www.dynamicscompanions.com
Dynamics Companions

- 83 -

www.blindsquirrelpublishing.com
© 2019 Blind Squirrel Publishing, LLC , All Rights Reserved

BLIND SQUIRREL
PUBLISHING

DYNAMICS COMPANIONS
BARE BONES CONFIGURATION GUIDE

CONFIGURING SALES ORDER MANAGEMENT WITHIN DYNAMICS 365 FOR FINANCE & OPERATIONS
MODULE 1: CONFIGURING SALES ORDER MANAGEMENT CONTROLS

Adding a Free Carrier Terms of Delivery code

How to do it...

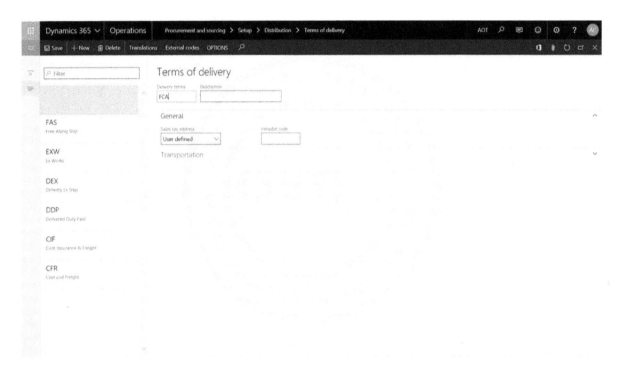

Step 2: Update the Delivery terms

We will then give our new record a **Delivery terms** code.

To do this we will just need to update the **Delivery terms** value.

For this example, we will want to set the **Delivery terms** to **FCA**.

www.dynamicscompanions.com
Dynamics Companions

- 84 -

www.blindsquirrelpublishing.com
© 2019 Blind Squirrel Publishing, LLC , All Rights Reserved

BLIND SQUIRREL
PUBLISHING

DYNAMICS COMPANIONS
BARE BONES CONFIGURATION GUIDE

CONFIGURING SALES ORDER MANAGEMENT WITHIN DYNAMICS 365 FOR FINANCE & OPERATIONS
MODULE 1: CONFIGURING SALES ORDER MANAGEMENT CONTROLS

Adding a Free Carrier Terms of Delivery code

How to do it...

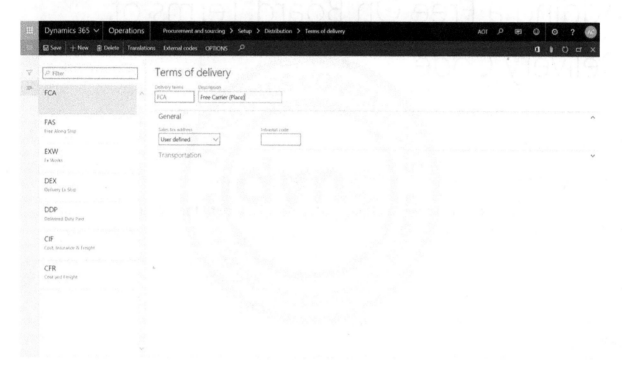

Step 3: Update the Description

And then we will give our Terms of delivery record a more detailed description so that the users can decipher the code.

To do this we will just need to update the **Description** value.

For this example, we will want to set the **Description** to **Free Carrier (Place)**.

dync
www.dynamicscompanions.com
Dynamics Companions

- 85 -

www.blindsquirrelpublishing.com
© 2019 Blind Squirrel Publishing, LLC , All Rights Reserved

BLIND SQUIRREL
PUBLISHING

DYNAMICS COMPANIONS
BARE BONES CONFIGURATION GUIDE

CONFIGURING SALES ORDER MANAGEMENT WITHIN DYNAMICS 365 FOR FINANCE & OPERATIONS
MODULE 1: CONFIGURING SALES ORDER MANAGEMENT CONTROLS

Adding a Free On Board Terms of Delivery Code

Finally we will want to add our last Terms of Delivery record for **Free On Board**.

How to do it...

Step 1: Click New

To do this we will want to create one last Terms of delivery record within the maintenance form.

Click on the **New** button.

Step 2: Update the Delivery terms

We will now give our Terms of delivery record a **Delivery terms** code.

Set the Delivery terms to FOB.

Step 3: Update the Description

Then we will want to give our new record a detailed **Description** that will give the users a better explanation of the code.

Set the Description to Free on Board.

DYNAMICS COMPANIONS
BARE BONES CONFIGURATION GUIDE

CONFIGURING SALES ORDER MANAGEMENT WITHIN DYNAMICS 365 FOR FINANCE & OPERATIONS
MODULE 1: CONFIGURING SALES ORDER MANAGEMENT CONTROLS

Adding a Free On Board Terms of Delivery Code

How to do it...

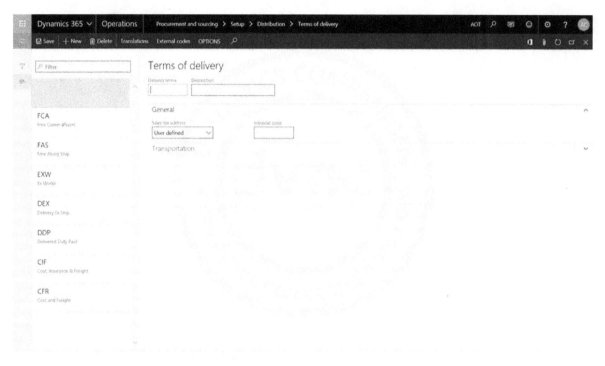

Step 1: Click New

To do this we will want to create one last Terms of delivery record within the maintenance form.

To do this just click on the **New** button.

dyn c

www.dynamicscompanions.com
Dynamics Companions

- 87 -

www.blindsquirrelpublishing.com
© 2019 Blind Squirrel Publishing, LLC , All Rights Reserved

BLIND SQUIRREL
PUBLISHING

DYNAMICS COMPANIONS
BARE BONES CONFIGURATION GUIDE

CONFIGURING SALES ORDER MANAGEMENT WITHIN DYNAMICS 365 FOR FINANCE & OPERATIONS
MODULE 1: CONFIGURING SALES ORDER MANAGEMENT CONTROLS

Adding a Free On Board Terms of Delivery Code

How to do it...

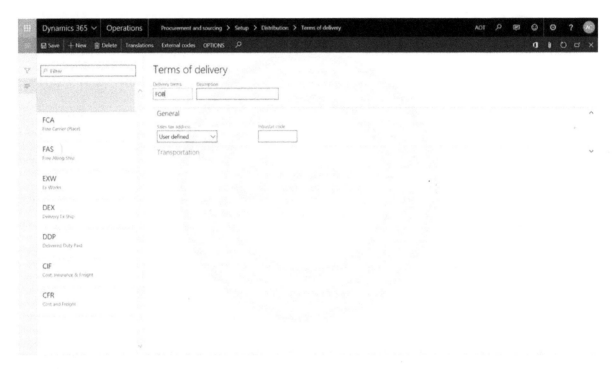

Step 2: Update the Delivery terms

We will now give our Terms of delivery record a **Delivery terms** code.

To do this we will just need to update the **Delivery terms** value.

For this example, we will want to set the **Delivery terms** to **FOB**.

dyn☐

www.dynamicscompanions.com
Dynamics Companions

- 88 -

www.blindsquirrelpublishing.com
© 2019 Blind Squirrel Publishing, LLC , All Rights Reserved

BLIND SQUIRREL
PUBLISHING

DYNAMICS COMPANIONS
BARE BONES CONFIGURATION GUIDE

CONFIGURING SALES ORDER MANAGEMENT WITHIN DYNAMICS 365 FOR FINANCE & OPERATIONS
MODULE 1: CONFIGURING SALES ORDER MANAGEMENT CONTROLS

Adding a Free On Board Terms of Delivery Code

How to do it...

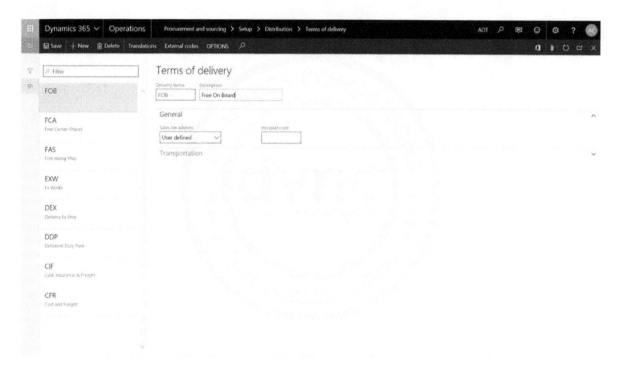

Step 3: Update the Description

Then we will want to give our new record a detailed **Description** that will give the users a better explanation of the code.

To do this we will just need to update the **Description** value.

For this example, we will want to set the **Description** to **Free on Board**.

dyn c
www.dynamicscompanions.com
Dynamics Companions

- 89 -

www.blindsquirrelpublishing.com
© 2019 Blind Squirrel Publishing, LLC , All Rights Reserved

BLIND SQUIRREL
PUBLISHING

DYNAMICS COMPANIONS
BARE BONES CONFIGURATION GUIDE

CONFIGURING SALES ORDER MANAGEMENT WITHIN DYNAMICS 365 FOR FINANCE & OPERATIONS
MODULE 1: CONFIGURING SALES ORDER MANAGEMENT CONTROLS

Adding a Free On Board Terms of Delivery Code

How to do it...

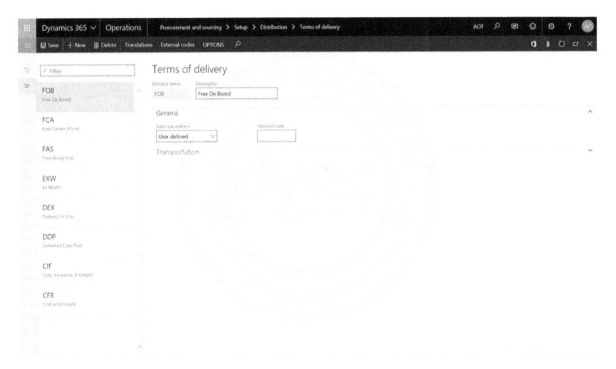

Step 3: Update the Description

After we have done and we can close out of the form.

www.dynamicscompanions.com
Dynamics Companions

- 90 -

www.blindsquirrelpublishing.com
© 2019 Blind Squirrel Publishing, LLC, All Rights Reserved

BLIND SQUIRREL
PUBLISHING

DYNAMICS COMPANIONS
BARE BONES CONFIGURATION GUIDE

CONFIGURING SALES ORDER MANAGEMENT WITHIN DYNAMICS 365 FOR FINANCE & OPERATIONS
MODULE 1: CONFIGURING SALES ORDER MANAGEMENT CONTROLS

Summary

Congratulations, you have now set up most of the different Terms of Delivery codes that we will want to use within the system as we are purchasing our products.

DYNAMICS COMPANIONS
BARE BONES CONFIGURATION GUIDE

CONFIGURING SALES ORDER MANAGEMENT WITHIN DYNAMICS 365 FOR FINANCE & OPERATIONS
MODULE 1: CONFIGURING SALES ORDER MANAGEMENT CONTROLS

Configuring Modes Of Delivery

Next we will want to configure some default **Modes Of Delivery** that we can assign to our Customers and Sales Orders which we will use to indicate how the products are going to be delivered.

Topics Covered

- Opening the Modes of delivery maintenance form

- Adding a Truck Mode of Delivery

- Adding an Air Mode of Delivery Code

- Adding a Rail Mode of Delivery code

- Adding an Ocean Mode of Delivery code

- Adding a Parcel Mode of Delivery code

- Adding a Customer Pickup Mode of Delivery code

- Summary

DYNAMICS COMPANIONS
BARE BONES CONFIGURATION GUIDE

CONFIGURING SALES ORDER MANAGEMENT WITHIN DYNAMICS 365 FOR FINANCE & OPERATIONS
MODULE 1: CONFIGURING SALES ORDER MANAGEMENT CONTROLS

Opening the Modes of delivery maintenance form

We will need to open up the maintenance form that we used to maintain the **Modes of delivery** codes within the system.

How to do it...

Step 1: Open the Modes of delivery form through the menu

We can get to the **Modes of delivery** form a couple of different ways. The first way is through the master menu.

Navigate to Sales and Marketing > Setup > Distribution > Modes of delivery.

Step 2: Open the Modes of delivery form through the menu search

Another way that we can find the **Modes of delivery** form is through the menu search feature.

Type in **modes** into the menu search and select **Modes of delivery**.

This will open up the **Modes of delivery** maintenance form.

If you have set up the Procurement and Sourcing module then you my notice that there are already a number of standard mode of delivery codes that are in this form. That is because they are shared between the modules.

www.dynamicscompanions.com
Dynamics Companions

- 93 -

www.blindsquirrelpublishing.com
© 2019 Blind Squirrel Publishing, LLC , All Rights Reserved

BLIND SQUIRREL
PUBLISHING

DYNAMICS COMPANIONS
BARE BONES CONFIGURATION GUIDE

CONFIGURING SALES ORDER MANAGEMENT WITHIN DYNAMICS 365 FOR FINANCE & OPERATIONS
MODULE 1: CONFIGURING SALES ORDER MANAGEMENT CONTROLS

Opening the Modes of delivery maintenance form

How to do it...

Step 1: Open the Modes of delivery form through the menu

We can get to the **Modes of delivery** form a couple of different ways. The first way is through the master menu.

To do this, open up the navigation panel, expand out the **Modules** and group, and click on **Sales and Marketing** to see all of the menu items that are available. Then click on the **Modes of delivery** menu item within the **Distribution** folder of the **Setup** group.

dync
Dynamics Companions

www.dynamicscompanions.com
Dynamics Companions

- 94 -

www.blindsquirrelpublishing.com
© 2019 Blind Squirrel Publishing, LLC , All Rights Reserved

BLIND SQUIRREL
PUBLISHING

DYNAMICS COMPANIONS
BARE BONES CONFIGURATION GUIDE

CONFIGURING SALES ORDER MANAGEMENT WITHIN DYNAMICS 365 FOR FINANCE & OPERATIONS
MODULE 1: CONFIGURING SALES ORDER MANAGEMENT CONTROLS

Opening the Modes of delivery maintenance form

How to do it...

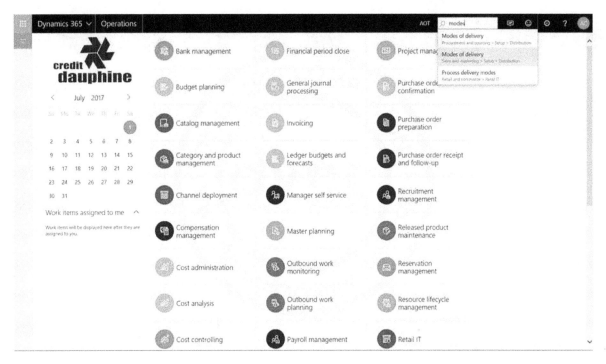

Step 2: Open the Modes of delivery form through the menu search

Another way that we can find the **Modes of delivery** form is through the menu search feature.

We can do this by clicking on the search icon in the header of the form (or by pressing **ALT+G**) and then type in **modes** into the search box. Then you will be able to select the **Modes of delivery** form from the dropdown list.

dyn c
www.dynamicscompanions.com
Dynamics Companions

- 95 -

www.blindsquirrelpublishing.com
© 2019 Blind Squirrel Publishing, LLC , All Rights Reserved

BLIND SQUIRREL
PUBLISHING

DYNAMICS COMPANIONS
BARE BONES CONFIGURATION GUIDE

CONFIGURING SALES ORDER MANAGEMENT WITHIN DYNAMICS 365 FOR FINANCE & OPERATIONS
MODULE 1: CONFIGURING SALES ORDER MANAGEMENT CONTROLS

Opening the Modes of delivery maintenance form

How to do it...

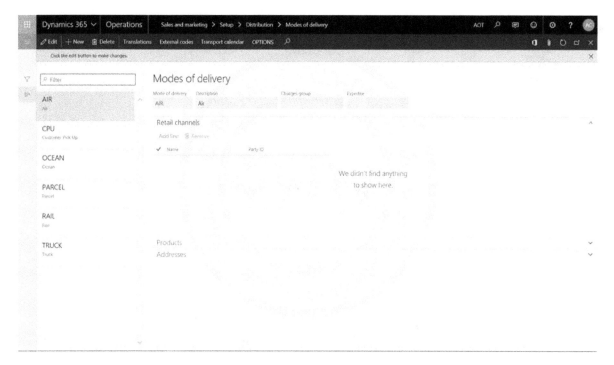

Step 2: Open the Modes of delivery form through the menu search

This will open up the **Modes of delivery** maintenance form.

If you have set up the Procurement and Sourcing module then you my notice that there are already a number of standard mode of delivery codes that are in this form. That is because they are shared between the modules.

dync
www.dynamicscompanions.com
Dynamics Companions

- 96 -

www.blindsquirrelpublishing.com
© 2019 Blind Squirrel Publishing, LLC , All Rights Reserved

BLIND SQUIRREL
PUBLISHING

DYNAMICS COMPANIONS
BARE BONES CONFIGURATION GUIDE

CONFIGURING SALES ORDER MANAGEMENT WITHIN DYNAMICS 365 FOR FINANCE & OPERATIONS
MODULE 1: CONFIGURING SALES ORDER MANAGEMENT CONTROLS

Adding a Truck Mode of Delivery

We will start off by adding our first Mode of Delivery record which will be for Truck based deliveries.

How to do it...

Step 1: Click New

If you don't have any terms of modes of delivery configured yet, then we will need to add them to the system.

To do this we will start off by creating a new Mode of delivery record within the maintenance form.

Click on the **New** button.

Step 2: Update the Mode of delivery

We will now want to give our record a **Mode of delivery** code that we can use to reference it within the system.

Set the Mode of delivery to TRUCK.

Step 3: Update the Description

And then we will want to give our Mode of delivery a description that will help the users understand the record's purpose.

Set the Description to Truck.

www.dynamicscompanions.com
Dynamics Companions

- 97 -

www.blindsquirrelpublishing.com
© 2019 Blind Squirrel Publishing, LLC , All Rights Reserved

BLIND SQUIRREL
PUBLISHING

DYNAMICS COMPANIONS
BARE BONES CONFIGURATION GUIDE

CONFIGURING SALES ORDER MANAGEMENT WITHIN DYNAMICS 365 FOR FINANCE & OPERATIONS
MODULE 1: CONFIGURING SALES ORDER MANAGEMENT CONTROLS

Adding a Truck Mode of Delivery

How to do it...

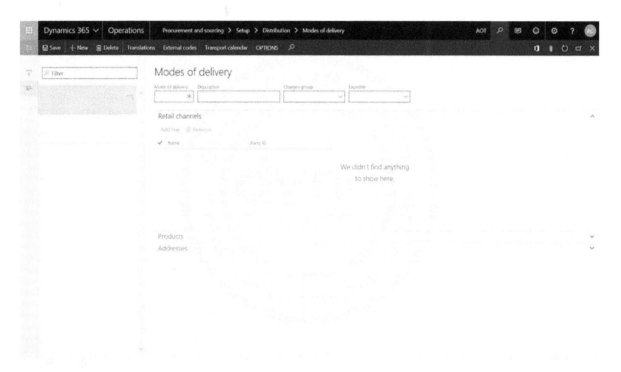

Step 1: Click New

If you don't have any terms of modes of delivery configured yet, then we will need to add them to the system.

To do this we will start off by creating a new Mode of delivery record within the maintenance form.

To do this just click on the **New** button.

dyn c
www.dynamicscompanions.com
Dynamics Companions

- 98 -

www.blindsquirrelpublishing.com
© 2019 Blind Squirrel Publishing, LLC , All Rights Reserved

BLIND SQUIRREL
PUBLISHING

DYNAMICS COMPANIONS
BARE BONES CONFIGURATION GUIDE

CONFIGURING SALES ORDER MANAGEMENT WITHIN DYNAMICS 365 FOR FINANCE & OPERATIONS
MODULE 1: CONFIGURING SALES ORDER MANAGEMENT CONTROLS

Adding a Truck Mode of Delivery

How to do it...

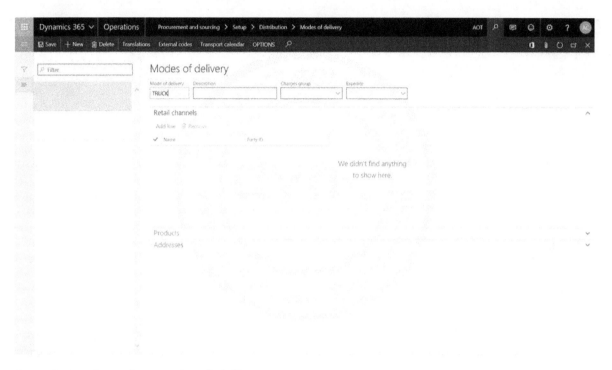

Step 2: Update the Mode of delivery

We will now want to give our record a **Mode of delivery** code that we can use to reference it within the system.

To do this we will just need to update the **Mode of delivery** value.

For this example, we will want to set the **Mode of delivery** to TRUCK.

dync
www.dynamicscompanions.com
Dynamics Companions

- 99 -

www.blindsquirrelpublishing.com
© 2019 Blind Squirrel Publishing, LLC , All Rights Reserved

BLIND SQUIRREL
PUBLISHING

DYNAMICS COMPANIONS
BARE BONES CONFIGURATION GUIDE

CONFIGURING SALES ORDER MANAGEMENT WITHIN DYNAMICS 365 FOR FINANCE & OPERATIONS
MODULE 1: CONFIGURING SALES ORDER MANAGEMENT CONTROLS

Adding a Truck Mode of Delivery

How to do it...

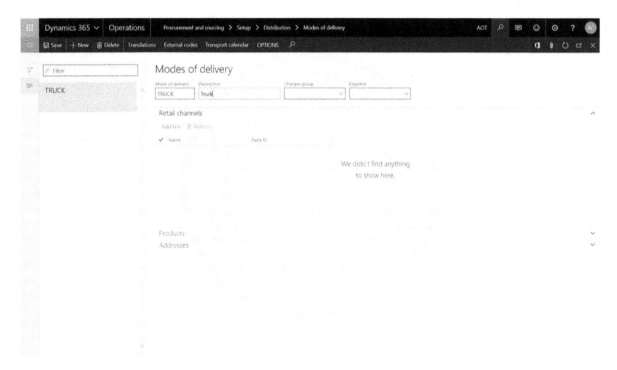

Step 3: Update the Description

And then we will want to give our Mode of delivery a description that will help the users understand the record's purpose.

To do this we will just need to update the **Description** value.

For this example, we will want to set the **Description** to **Truck**.

www.dynamicscompanions.com
Dynamics Companions

- 100 -

www.blindsquirrelpublishing.com
© 2019 Blind Squirrel Publishing, LLC , All Rights Reserved

BLIND SQUIRREL
PUBLISHING

DYNAMICS COMPANIONS
BARE BONES CONFIGURATION GUIDE

CONFIGURING SALES ORDER MANAGEMENT WITHIN DYNAMICS 365 FOR FINANCE & OPERATIONS
MODULE 1: CONFIGURING SALES ORDER MANAGEMENT CONTROLS

Adding an Air Mode of Delivery Code

Now we will add another Mode of Delivery code, this time we will add one for delivery by Air.

How to do it...

Step 1: Click New

We will need to create a new Mode of Delivery record.

Click on the **New** button.

Step 2: Update the Mode of delivery

Next we will want to give our new record a **Mode of delivery** code to reference it by.

Set the Mode of delivery to AIR.

Step 3: Update the Description

Then we will give our Mode of delivery a description for the users.

Set the Description to Air.

DYNAMICS COMPANIONS
BARE BONES CONFIGURATION GUIDE

CONFIGURING SALES ORDER MANAGEMENT WITHIN DYNAMICS 365 FOR FINANCE & OPERATIONS
MODULE 1: CONFIGURING SALES ORDER MANAGEMENT CONTROLS

Adding an Air Mode of Delivery Code

How to do it...

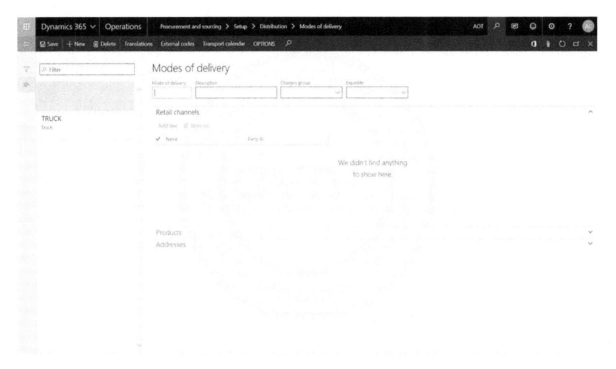

Step 1: Click New

We will need to create a new Mode of Delivery record.

To do this just click on the **New** button.

www.dynamicscompanions.com
Dynamics Companions

- 102 -

www.blindsquirrelpublishing.com
© 2019 Blind Squirrel Publishing, LLC, All Rights Reserved

BLIND SQUIRREL
PUBLISHING

DYNAMICS COMPANIONS
BARE BONES CONFIGURATION GUIDE

CONFIGURING SALES ORDER MANAGEMENT WITHIN DYNAMICS 365 FOR FINANCE & OPERATIONS
MODULE 1: CONFIGURING SALES ORDER MANAGEMENT CONTROLS

Adding an Air Mode of Delivery Code

How to do it...

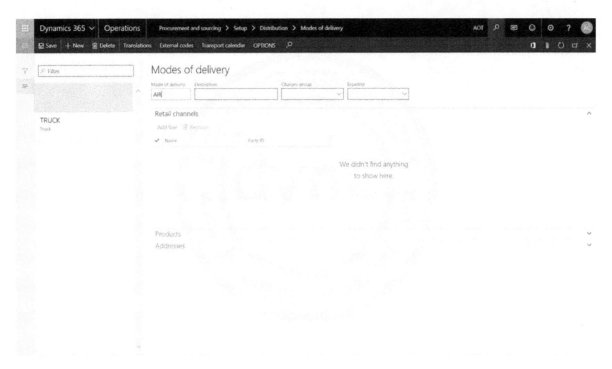

Step 2: Update the Mode of delivery

Next we will want to give our new record a **Mode of delivery** code to reference it by.

To do this we will just need to update the **Mode of delivery** value.

For this example, we will want to set the **Mode of delivery** to **AIR**.

dyn c
www.dynamicscompanions.com
Dynamics Companions

- 103 -

www.blindsquirrelpublishing.com
© 2019 Blind Squirrel Publishing, LLC, All Rights Reserved

BLIND SQUIRREL
PUBLISHING

DYNAMICS COMPANIONS
BARE BONES CONFIGURATION GUIDE

CONFIGURING SALES ORDER MANAGEMENT WITHIN DYNAMICS 365 FOR FINANCE & OPERATIONS
MODULE 1: CONFIGURING SALES ORDER MANAGEMENT CONTROLS

Adding an Air Mode of Delivery Code

How to do it...

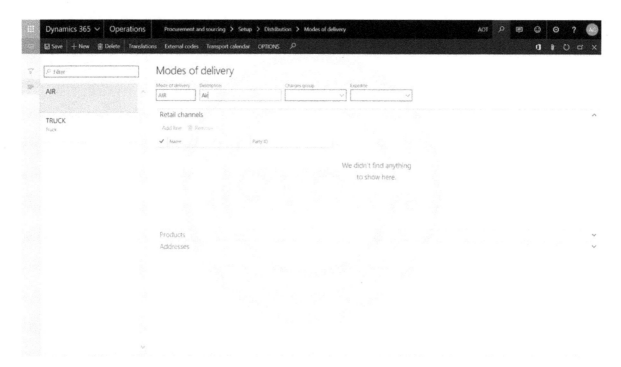

Step 3: Update the Description

Then we will give our Mode of delivery a description for the users.

To do this we will just need to update the **Description** value.

For this example, we will want to set the **Description** to **Air**.

www.dynamicscompanions.com
Dynamics Companions

- 104 -

www.blindsquirrelpublishing.com
© 2019 Blind Squirrel Publishing, LLC , All Rights Reserved

BLIND SQUIRREL
PUBLISHING

DYNAMICS COMPANIONS
BARE BONES CONFIGURATION GUIDE

CONFIGURING SALES ORDER MANAGEMENT WITHIN DYNAMICS 365 FOR FINANCE & OPERATIONS
MODULE 1: CONFIGURING SALES ORDER MANAGEMENT CONTROLS

Adding a Rail Mode of Delivery code

Now we will add a new Mode of Delivery for all of our Rail deliveries that we may need to srack.

How to do it...

Step 1: Click New

We will do this by adding a new record to the Modes of delivery form.

Click on the **New** button.

Step 2: Update the Mode of delivery

We will add a **Mode of delivery** code to the record.

Set the Mode of delivery to RAIL'.

Step 3: Update the Description

And then we will want to add a **Description** to the new Mode of delivery record.

Set the Description to Rail.

dync
www.dynamicscompanions.com
Dynamics Companions

- 105 -

www.blindsquirrelpublishing.com
© 2019 Blind Squirrel Publishing, LLC , All Rights Reserved

BLIND SQUIRREL
PUBLISHING

DYNAMICS COMPANIONS
BARE BONES CONFIGURATION GUIDE

CONFIGURING SALES ORDER MANAGEMENT WITHIN DYNAMICS 365 FOR FINANCE & OPERATIONS
MODULE 1: CONFIGURING SALES ORDER MANAGEMENT CONTROLS

Adding a Rail Mode of Delivery code

How to do it...

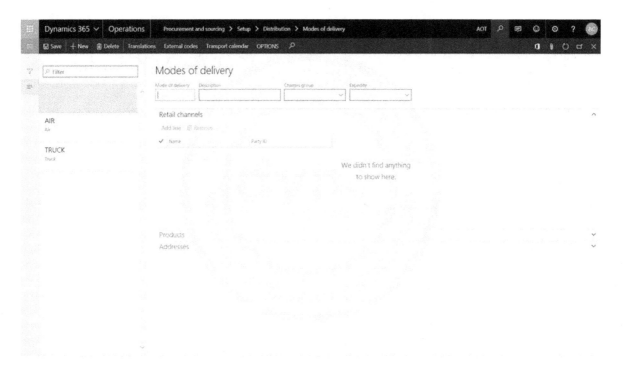

Step 1: Click New

We will do this by adding a new record to the Modes of delivery form.

To do this just click on the **New** button.

dync
DYNAMICS COMPANIONS

www.dynamicscompanions.com
Dynamics Companions

- 106 -

www.blindsquirrelpublishing.com
© 2019 Blind Squirrel Publishing, LLC , All Rights Reserved

BLIND SQUIRREL
PUBLISHING

DYNAMICS COMPANIONS
BARE BONES CONFIGURATION GUIDE

CONFIGURING SALES ORDER MANAGEMENT WITHIN DYNAMICS 365 FOR FINANCE & OPERATIONS
MODULE 1: CONFIGURING SALES ORDER MANAGEMENT CONTROLS

Adding a Rail Mode of Delivery code

How to do it...

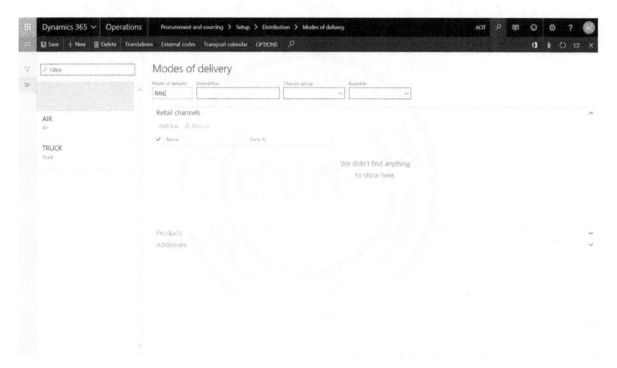

Step 2: Update the Mode of delivery

We will add a **Mode of delivery** code to the record.

To do this we will just need to update the **Mode of delivery** value.

For this example, we will want to set the **Mode of delivery** to **RAIL'**.

dyn c
www.dynamicscompanions.com
Dynamics Companions

- 107 -

www.blindsquirrelpublishing.com
© 2019 Blind Squirrel Publishing, LLC, All Rights Reserved

BLIND SQUIRREL
PUBLISHING

DYNAMICS COMPANIONS
BARE BONES CONFIGURATION GUIDE

CONFIGURING SALES ORDER MANAGEMENT WITHIN DYNAMICS 365 FOR FINANCE & OPERATIONS
MODULE 1: CONFIGURING SALES ORDER MANAGEMENT CONTROLS

Adding a Rail Mode of Delivery code

How to do it...

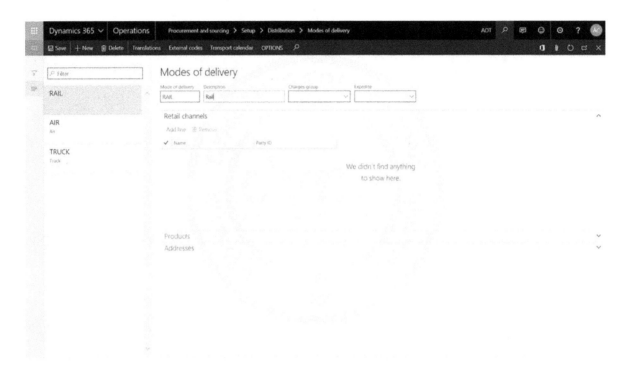

Step 3: Update the Description

And then we will want to add a **Description** to the new Mode of delivery record.

To do this we will just need to update the **Description** value.

For this example, we will want to set the **Description** to **Rail**.

www.dynamicscompanions.com
Dynamics Companions

- 108 -

www.blindsquirrelpublishing.com
© 2019 Blind Squirrel Publishing, LLC , All Rights Reserved

BLIND SQUIRREL
PUBLISHING

DYNAMICS COMPANIONS
BARE BONES CONFIGURATION GUIDE

CONFIGURING SALES ORDER MANAGEMENT WITHIN DYNAMICS 365 FOR FINANCE & OPERATIONS
MODULE 1: CONFIGURING SALES ORDER MANAGEMENT CONTROLS

Adding an Ocean Mode of Delivery code

We will add another **Mode of delivery** record to the system for **Ocean** deliveries.

How to do it...

Step 1: Click New

We will need to create a new record within the Modes of delivery form.

Click on the **New** button.

Step 2: Update the Mode of delivery

Now we will want to assign our record a **Mode of delivery** code.

Set the Mode of delivery to OCEAN.

Step 3: Update the Description

And then we will want to give our record a **Description** that the users can apprciate.

Set the Description to Ocean.

dync
www.dynamicscompanions.com
Dynamics Companions

- 109 -

www.blindsquirrelpublishing.com
© 2019 Blind Squirrel Publishing, LLC , All Rights Reserved

BLIND SQUIRREL
PUBLISHING

DYNAMICS COMPANIONS
BARE BONES CONFIGURATION GUIDE

CONFIGURING SALES ORDER MANAGEMENT WITHIN DYNAMICS 365 FOR FINANCE & OPERATIONS
MODULE 1: CONFIGURING SALES ORDER MANAGEMENT CONTROLS

Adding an Ocean Mode of Delivery code

How to do it...

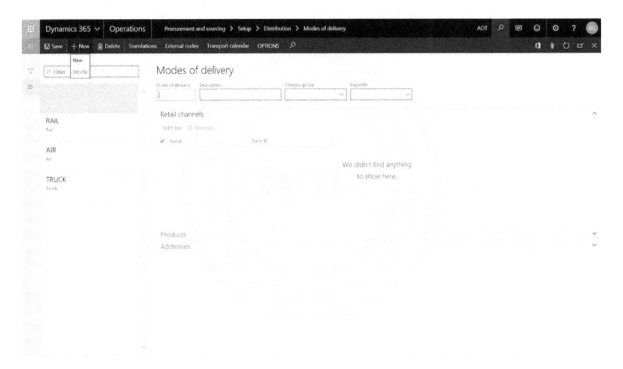

Step 1: Click New

We will need to create a new record within the Modes of delivery form.

To do this just click on the **New** button.

dyn c
www.dynamicscompanions.com
Dynamics Companions

- 110 -

www.blindsquirrelpublishing.com
© 2019 Blind Squirrel Publishing, LLC , All Rights Reserved

BLIND SQUIRREL
PUBLISHING

DYNAMICS COMPANIONS
BARE BONES CONFIGURATION GUIDE

CONFIGURING SALES ORDER MANAGEMENT WITHIN DYNAMICS 365 FOR FINANCE & OPERATIONS
MODULE 1: CONFIGURING SALES ORDER MANAGEMENT CONTROLS

Adding an Ocean Mode of Delivery code

How to do it...

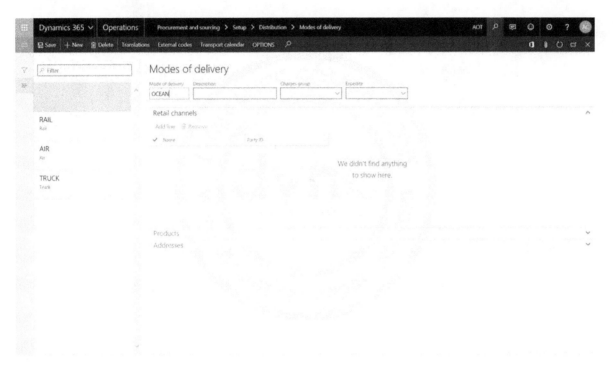

Step 2: Update the Mode of delivery

Now we will want to assign our record a **Mode of delivery** code.

To do this we will just need to update the **Mode of delivery** value.

For this example, we will want to set the **Mode of delivery** to **OCEAN**.

DYNAMICS COMPANIONS
BARE BONES CONFIGURATION GUIDE

CONFIGURING SALES ORDER MANAGEMENT WITHIN DYNAMICS 365 FOR FINANCE & OPERATIONS
MODULE 1: CONFIGURING SALES ORDER MANAGEMENT CONTROLS

Adding an Ocean Mode of Delivery code

How to do it...

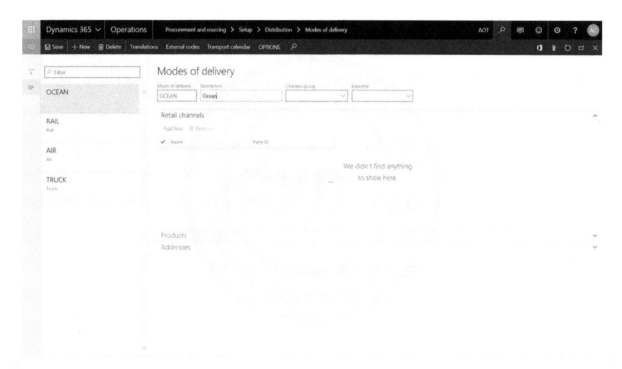

Step 3: Update the Description

And then we will want to give our record a **Description** that the users can apprciate.

To do this we will just need to update the **Description** value.

For this example, we will want to set the **Description** to **Ocean**.

www.dynamicscompanions.com
Dynamics Companions

- 112 -

www.blindsquirrelpublishing.com
© 2019 Blind Squirrel Publishing, LLC , All Rights Reserved

BLIND SQUIRREL
PUBLISHING

DYNAMICS COMPANIONS
BARE BONES CONFIGURATION GUIDE

CONFIGURING SALES ORDER MANAGEMENT WITHIN DYNAMICS 365 FOR FINANCE & OPERATIONS
MODULE 1: CONFIGURING SALES ORDER MANAGEMENT CONTROLS

Adding a Parcel Mode of Delivery code

Now we will add another **Mode of delivery** record for all of our **Parcel** deliveries.

How to do it...

Step 1: Click New

We will need to add a new Mode of delivery record.

Click on the **New** button.

Step 2: Update the Mode of delivery

We will then want to give our new record a **Mode of delivery** code.

Set the Mode of delivery to PARCEL.

Step 3: Update the Description

Then we will want to give record a **Description** for the mode of delivery.

Set the Description to Parcel.

dync
www.dynamicscompanions.com
Dynamics Companions

- 113 -

www.blindsquirrelpublishing.com
© 2019 Blind Squirrel Publishing, LLC, All Rights Reserved

BLIND SQUIRREL
PUBLISHING

DYNAMICS COMPANIONS
BARE BONES CONFIGURATION GUIDE

CONFIGURING SALES ORDER MANAGEMENT WITHIN DYNAMICS 365 FOR FINANCE & OPERATIONS
MODULE 1: CONFIGURING SALES ORDER MANAGEMENT CONTROLS

Adding a Parcel Mode of Delivery code

How to do it...

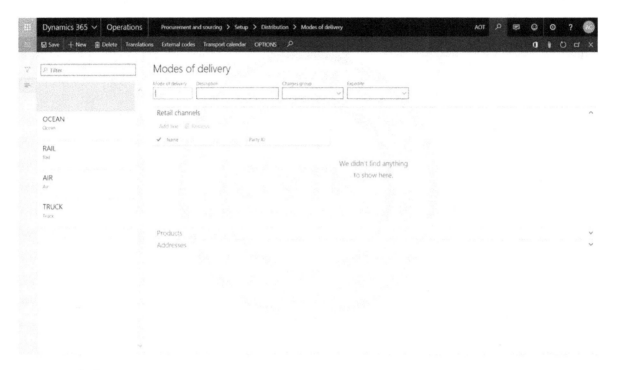

Step 1: Click New

We will need to add a new Mode of delivery record.

To do this just click on the **New** button.

www.dynamicscompanions.com
Dynamics Companions

- 114 -

www.blindsquirrelpublishing.com
© 2019 Blind Squirrel Publishing, LLC , All Rights Reserved

BLIND SQUIRREL
PUBLISHING

DYNAMICS COMPANIONS
BARE BONES CONFIGURATION GUIDE

CONFIGURING SALES ORDER MANAGEMENT WITHIN DYNAMICS 365 FOR FINANCE & OPERATIONS
MODULE 1: CONFIGURING SALES ORDER MANAGEMENT CONTROLS

Adding a Parcel Mode of Delivery code

How to do it...

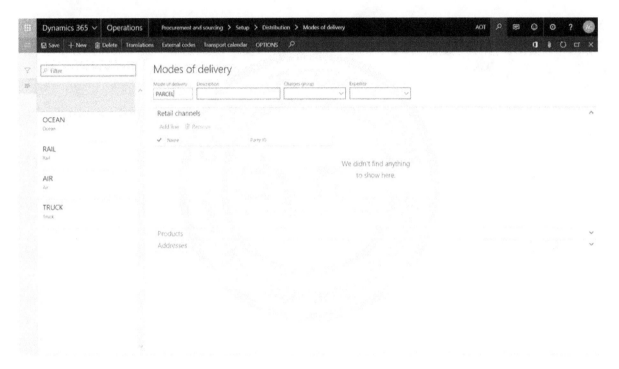

Step 2: Update the Mode of delivery

We will then want to give our new record a **Mode of delivery** code.

To do this we will just need to update the **Mode of delivery** value.

For this example, we will want to set the **Mode of delivery** to **PARCEL**.

dync

www.dynamicscompanions.com
Dynamics Companions

- 115 -

www.blindsquirrelpublishing.com
© 2019 Blind Squirrel Publishing, LLC , All Rights Reserved

BLIND SQUIRREL
PUBLISHING

DYNAMICS COMPANIONS
BARE BONES CONFIGURATION GUIDE

CONFIGURING SALES ORDER MANAGEMENT WITHIN DYNAMICS 365 FOR FINANCE & OPERATIONS
MODULE 1: CONFIGURING SALES ORDER MANAGEMENT CONTROLS

Adding a Parcel Mode of Delivery code

How to do it...

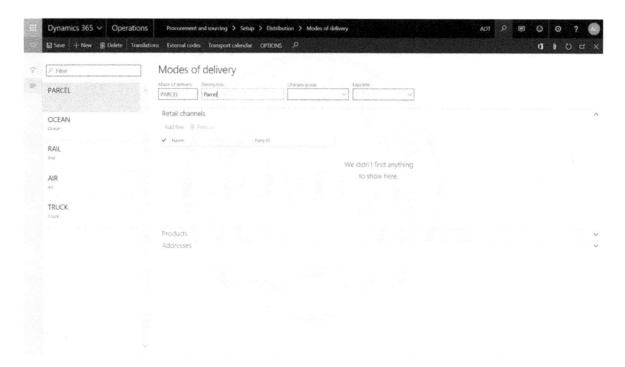

Step 3: Update the Description

Then we will want to give record a **Description** for the mode of delivery.

To do this we will just need to update the **Description** value.

For this example, we will want to set the **Description** to **Parcel**.

dync
www.dynamicscompanions.com
Dynamics Companions

- 116 -

www.blindsquirrelpublishing.com
© 2019 Blind Squirrel Publishing, LLC , All Rights Reserved

BLIND SQUIRREL
PUBLISHING

DYNAMICS COMPANIONS
BARE BONES CONFIGURATION GUIDE

CONFIGURING SALES ORDER MANAGEMENT WITHIN DYNAMICS 365 FOR FINANCE & OPERATIONS
MODULE 1: CONFIGURING SALES ORDER MANAGEMENT CONTROLS

Adding a Customer Pickup Mode of Delivery code

We will add one last **Mode of delivery** record for **Customer Pickup** record.

How to do it...

Step 1: Click New

We will add one last Mode of delivery record.

Click on the **New** button.

Step 2: Update the Mode of delivery

We will now want to give our record a **Mode of delivery** code to reference it.

Set the Mode of delivery to CPU.

Step 3: Update the Description

And then we will want to give our new record a better **Description** for the users.

Set the Description to Customer Pick Up.

www.dynamicscompanions.com
Dynamics Companions

- 117 -

www.blindsquirrelpublishing.com
© 2019 Blind Squirrel Publishing, LLC, All Rights Reserved

BLIND SQUIRREL
PUBLISHING

DYNAMICS COMPANIONS
BARE BONES CONFIGURATION GUIDE

CONFIGURING SALES ORDER MANAGEMENT WITHIN DYNAMICS 365 FOR FINANCE & OPERATIONS
MODULE 1: CONFIGURING SALES ORDER MANAGEMENT CONTROLS

Adding a Customer Pickup Mode of Delivery code

How to do it...

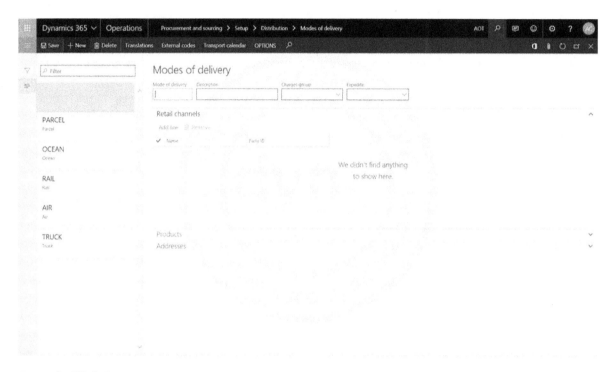

Step 1: Click New

We will add one last Mode of delivery record.

To do this just click on the **New** button.

www.dynamicscompanions.com
Dynamics Companions

- 118 -

www.blindsquirrelpublishing.com
© 2019 Blind Squirrel Publishing, LLC , All Rights Reserved

BLIND SQUIRREL
PUBLISHING

DYNAMICS COMPANIONS
BARE BONES CONFIGURATION GUIDE

CONFIGURING SALES ORDER MANAGEMENT WITHIN DYNAMICS 365 FOR FINANCE & OPERATIONS
MODULE 1: CONFIGURING SALES ORDER MANAGEMENT CONTROLS

Adding a Customer Pickup Mode of Delivery code

How to do it...

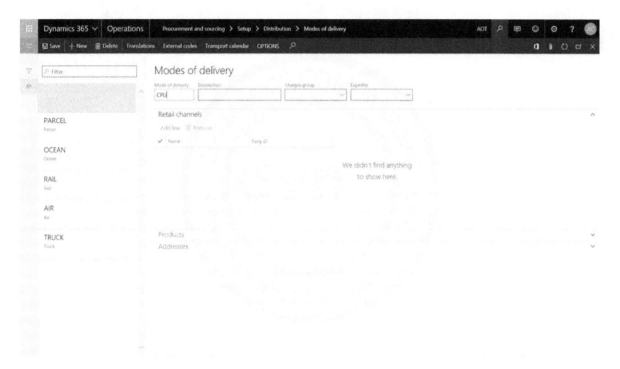

Step 2: Update the Mode of delivery

We will now want to give our record a **Mode of delivery** code to reference it.

To do this we will just need to update the **Mode of delivery** value.

For this example, we will want to set the **Mode of delivery** to **CPU**.

www.dynamicscompanions.com
Dynamics Companions

- 119 -

www.blindsquirrelpublishing.com
© 2019 Blind Squirrel Publishing, LLC , All Rights Reserved

BLIND SQUIRREL
PUBLISHING

DYNAMICS COMPANIONS
BARE BONES CONFIGURATION GUIDE

CONFIGURING SALES ORDER MANAGEMENT WITHIN DYNAMICS 365 FOR FINANCE & OPERATIONS
MODULE 1: CONFIGURING SALES ORDER MANAGEMENT CONTROLS

Adding a Customer Pickup Mode of Delivery code

How to do it...

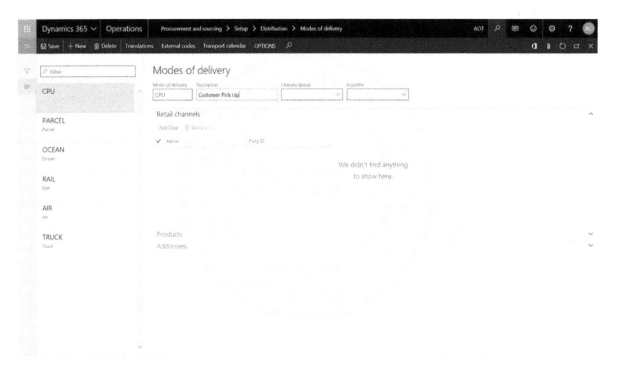

Step 3: Update the Description

And then we will want to give our new record a better **Description** for the users.

To do this we will just need to update the **Description** value.

For this example, we will want to set the **Description** to **Customer Pick Up**.

dync
dynamics companions

www.dynamicscompanions.com
Dynamics Companions

- 120 -

www.blindsquirrelpublishing.com
© 2019 Blind Squirrel Publishing, LLC , All Rights Reserved

BLIND SQUIRREL
PUBLISHING

DYNAMICS COMPANIONS
BARE BONES CONFIGURATION GUIDE

CONFIGURING SALES ORDER MANAGEMENT WITHIN DYNAMICS 365 FOR FINANCE & OPERATIONS
MODULE 1: CONFIGURING SALES ORDER MANAGEMENT CONTROLS

Adding a Customer Pickup Mode of Delivery code

How to do it...

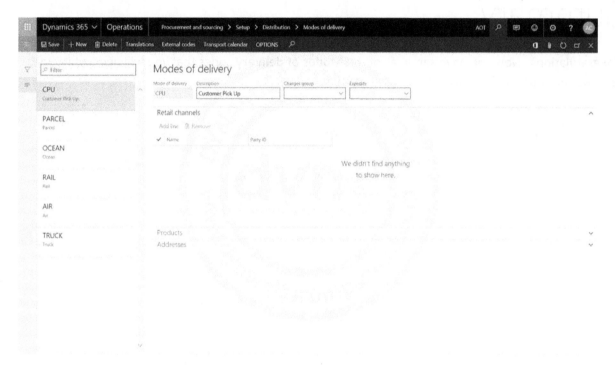

Step 3: Update the Description

After we have done that we can close out of the form.

www.dynamicscompanions.com
Dynamics Companions

- 121 -

www.blindsquirrelpublishing.com
© 2019 Blind Squirrel Publishing, LLC, All Rights Reserved

BLIND SQUIRREL
PUBLISHING

DYNAMICS COMPANIONS
BARE BONES CONFIGURATION GUIDE

CONFIGURING SALES ORDER MANAGEMENT WITHIN DYNAMICS 365 FOR FINANCE & OPERATIONS
MODULE 1: CONFIGURING SALES ORDER MANAGEMENT CONTROLS

Summary

Congratulations. Now you have set up all of the **Modes of delivery** codes that you will need while you are tracking your purchase orders within the system.

DYNAMICS COMPANIONS
BARE BONES CONFIGURATION GUIDE

CONFIGURING SALES ORDER MANAGEMENT WITHIN DYNAMICS 365 FOR FINANCE & OPERATIONS
MODULE 1: CONFIGURING SALES ORDER MANAGEMENT CONTROLS

Configuring Sales Order Origin Codes

Now we will configure some **Sales Origin Codes** which we will use to indicate how the order was received. This is a great way to segregate out our orders into different order channels so that we can see what is the most active ordering method.

Topics Covered

- Opening the Sales Origin maintenance form

- Creating an Email Sales Origin code

- Creating an Amazon Sales origin code

- Creating an Trade Show Sales origin code

- Creating an Phone Sales origin code

- Creating an Mail Sales origin code

- Creating an Website Sales origin code

- Creating an Fax Sales origin code

- Now we will configure some **Sales Origin Codes** which we will use to indicate how the order was received. This is a great way to segregate out our orders into different order channels so that we can see what is the most active ordering method.

 www.dynamicscompanions.com
Dynamics Companions

- 123 -

www.blindsquirrelpublishing.com
© 2019 Blind Squirrel Publishing, LLC , All Rights Reserved

BLIND SQUIRREL
PUBLISHING

DYNAMICS COMPANIONS
BARE BONES CONFIGURATION GUIDE

CONFIGURING SALES ORDER MANAGEMENT WITHIN DYNAMICS 365 FOR FINANCE & OPERATIONS
MODULE 1: CONFIGURING SALES ORDER MANAGEMENT CONTROLS

Opening the Sales Origin maintenance form

We will need to open up the maintenance form that we used to maintain the **Sales origin** codes within the system.

How to do it...

Step 1: Open the Sales origin form through the menu

We can get to the **Sales origin** form a couple of different ways. The first way is through the master menu.

Navigate to Sales and marketing > Setup > Sales orders > Sales origin.

Step 2: Open the Sales origin form through the menu search

Another way that we can find the **Sales origin** form is through the menu search feature.

Type in **sales orig** into the menu search and select **Sales origin**.

DYNAMICS COMPANIONS
BARE BONES CONFIGURATION GUIDE

CONFIGURING SALES ORDER MANAGEMENT WITHIN DYNAMICS 365 FOR FINANCE & OPERATIONS
MODULE 1: CONFIGURING SALES ORDER MANAGEMENT CONTROLS

Opening the Sales Origin maintenance form

How to do it...

Step 1: Open the Sales origin form through the menu

We can get to the **Sales origin** form a couple of different ways. The first way is through the master menu.

To do this, open up the navigation panel, expand out the **Modules** and group, and click on **Sales and marketing** to see all of the menu items that are available. Then click on the **Sales origin** menu item within the **Sales orders** folder of the **Setup** group.

dyn c
www.dynamicscompanions.com
Dynamics Companions

- 125 -

www.blindsquirrelpublishing.com
© 2019 Blind Squirrel Publishing, LLC, All Rights Reserved

BLIND SQUIRREL
PUBLISHING

DYNAMICS COMPANIONS
BARE BONES CONFIGURATION GUIDE

CONFIGURING SALES ORDER MANAGEMENT WITHIN DYNAMICS 365 FOR FINANCE & OPERATIONS
MODULE 1: CONFIGURING SALES ORDER MANAGEMENT CONTROLS

Opening the Sales Origin maintenance form

How to do it...

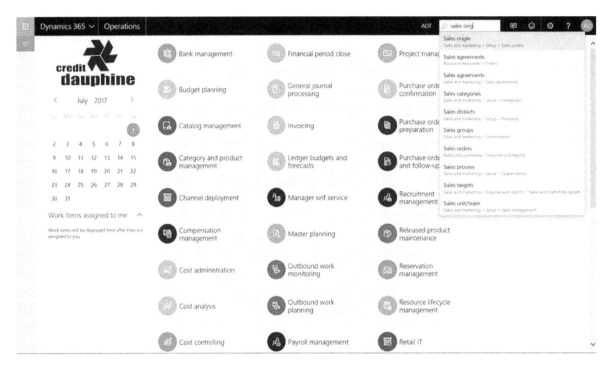

Step 2: Open the Sales origin form through the menu search

Another way that we can find the **Sales origin** form is through the menu search feature.

We can do this by clicking on the search icon in the header of the form (or by pressing **ALT+G**) and then type in **sales orig** into the search box. Then you will be able to select the **Sales origin** form from the dropdown list.

dync
www.dynamicscompanions.com
Dynamics Companions

- 126 -

www.blindsquirrelpublishing.com
© 2019 Blind Squirrel Publishing, LLC , All Rights Reserved

BLIND SQUIRREL
PUBLISHING

DYNAMICS COMPANIONS
BARE BONES CONFIGURATION GUIDE

CONFIGURING SALES ORDER MANAGEMENT WITHIN DYNAMICS 365 FOR FINANCE & OPERATIONS
MODULE 1: CONFIGURING SALES ORDER MANAGEMENT CONTROLS

Opening the Sales Origin maintenance form

How to do it...

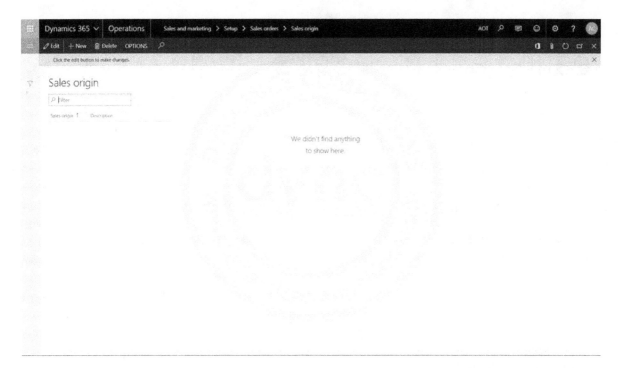

Step 2: Open the Sales origin form through the menu search

This will open up the **Sales origin** maintenance form where we will be able to configure all of the different origination channels for our sales orders.

dync
www.dynamicscompanions.com
Dynamics Companions

- 127 -

www.blindsquirrelpublishing.com
© 2019 Blind Squirrel Publishing, LLC, All Rights Reserved

BLIND SQUIRREL
PUBLISHING

DYNAMICS COMPANIONS
BARE BONES CONFIGURATION GUIDE

CONFIGURING SALES ORDER MANAGEMENT WITHIN DYNAMICS 365 FOR FINANCE & OPERATIONS
MODULE 1: CONFIGURING SALES ORDER MANAGEMENT CONTROLS

Creating an Email Sales Origin code

Now we can start creating new **Sales origin** codes.

We will start off by creating a code that is used to identify orders that come in through email.

How to do it...

Step 1: Click on the New button

To do this we will start off by creating a new Sales origin code record.

Click on the **New** button.

Step 2: Update the Sales origin

We will then want to give out new code a Sales origin code to easily refer to it.

Set the Sales origin to EMAIL.

Step 3: Update the Description

And then we will want to add a less formal Description for the code.

Set the Description to E-mail.

 www.dynamicscompanions.com
Dynamics Companions

- 128 -

DYNAMICS COMPANIONS
BARE BONES CONFIGURATION GUIDE

CONFIGURING SALES ORDER MANAGEMENT WITHIN DYNAMICS 365 FOR FINANCE & OPERATIONS
MODULE 1: CONFIGURING SALES ORDER MANAGEMENT CONTROLS

Creating an Email Sales Origin code

How to do it...

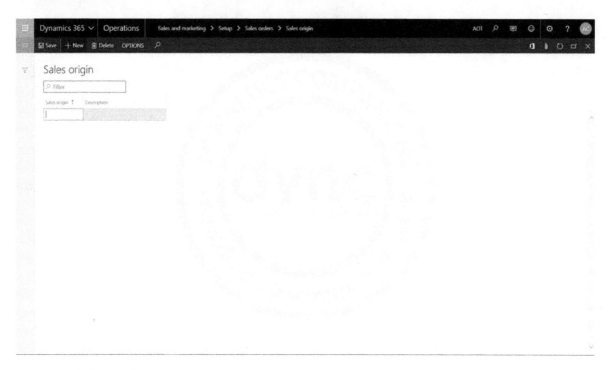

Step 1: Click on the New button

To do this we will start off by creating a new Sales origin code record.

To do this just click on the **New** button.

www.dynamicscompanions.com
Dynamics Companions

- 129 -

www.blindsquirrelpublishing.com
© 2019 Blind Squirrel Publishing, LLC , All Rights Reserved

BLIND SQUIRREL
PUBLISHING

DYNAMICS COMPANIONS
BARE BONES CONFIGURATION GUIDE

CONFIGURING SALES ORDER MANAGEMENT WITHIN DYNAMICS 365 FOR FINANCE & OPERATIONS
MODULE 1: CONFIGURING SALES ORDER MANAGEMENT CONTROLS

Creating an Email Sales Origin code

How to do it...

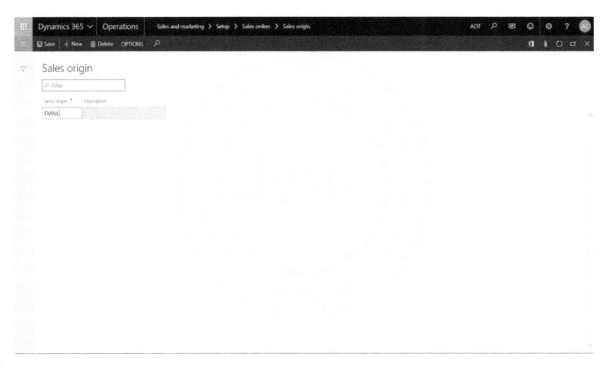

Step 2: Update the Sales origin

We will then want to give out new code a Sales origin code to easily refer to it.

To do this just update the **Sales origin** value.

This time, we will want to set the **Sales origin** to **EMAIL**.

dync
www.dynamicscompanions.com
Dynamics Companions

- 130 -

www.blindsquirrelpublishing.com
© 2019 Blind Squirrel Publishing, LLC , All Rights Reserved

BLIND SQUIRREL
PUBLISHING

DYNAMICS COMPANIONS
BARE BONES CONFIGURATION GUIDE

CONFIGURING SALES ORDER MANAGEMENT WITHIN DYNAMICS 365 FOR FINANCE & OPERATIONS
MODULE 1: CONFIGURING SALES ORDER MANAGEMENT CONTROLS

Creating an Email Sales Origin code

How to do it...

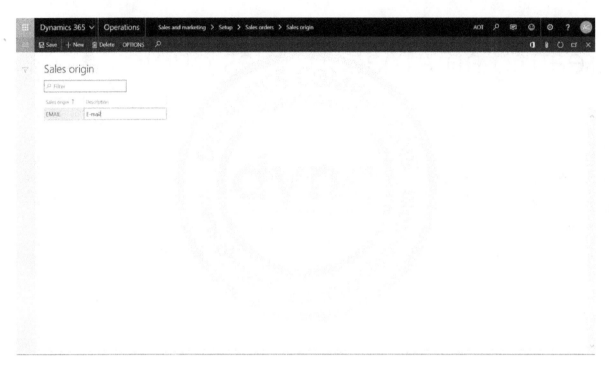

Step 3: Update the Description

And then we will want to add a less formal Description for the code.

To do this just update the **Description** value.

This time, we will want to set the **Description** to **E-mail**.

dync
www.dynamicscompanions.com
Dynamics Companions

- 131 -

www.blindsquirrelpublishing.com
© 2019 Blind Squirrel Publishing, LLC , All Rights Reserved

BLIND SQUIRREL
PUBLISHING

DYNAMICS COMPANIONS
BARE BONES CONFIGURATION GUIDE

CONFIGURING SALES ORDER MANAGEMENT WITHIN DYNAMICS 365 FOR FINANCE & OPERATIONS
MODULE 1: CONFIGURING SALES ORDER MANAGEMENT CONTROLS

Creating an Amazon Sales origin code

Next we will create a code to identify all of the orders that originate from Amazon.

How to do it...

Step 1: Click on the New button

We will want to go ahead and create a new record within the Sales origin table.

Click on the **New** button.

Step 2: Update the Sales origin and update the Description

Then we will be able to add a code and description to our new record.

Set the Sales origin to AMAZON and set the Description to Amazon.

DYNAMICS COMPANIONS
BARE BONES CONFIGURATION GUIDE

CONFIGURING SALES ORDER MANAGEMENT WITHIN DYNAMICS 365 FOR FINANCE & OPERATIONS
MODULE 1: CONFIGURING SALES ORDER MANAGEMENT CONTROLS

Creating an Amazon Sales origin code

How to do it...

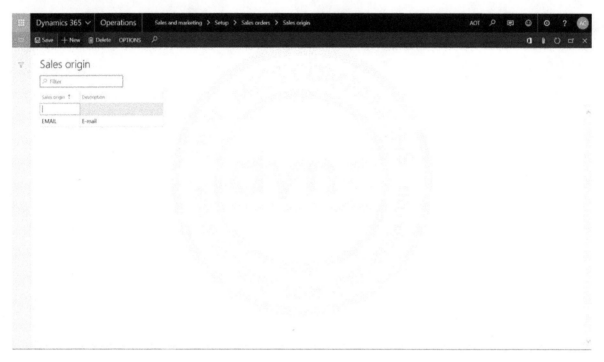

Step 1: Click on the New button

We will want to go ahead and create a new record within the Sales origin table.

To do this all we need to do is click on the **New** button.

www.dynamicscompanions.com
Dynamics Companions

- 133 -

www.blindsquirrelpublishing.com
© 2019 Blind Squirrel Publishing, LLC , All Rights Reserved

BLIND SQUIRREL
PUBLISHING

DYNAMICS COMPANIONS
BARE BONES CONFIGURATION GUIDE

CONFIGURING SALES ORDER MANAGEMENT WITHIN DYNAMICS 365 FOR FINANCE & OPERATIONS
MODULE 1: CONFIGURING SALES ORDER MANAGEMENT CONTROLS

Creating an Amazon Sales origin code

How to do it...

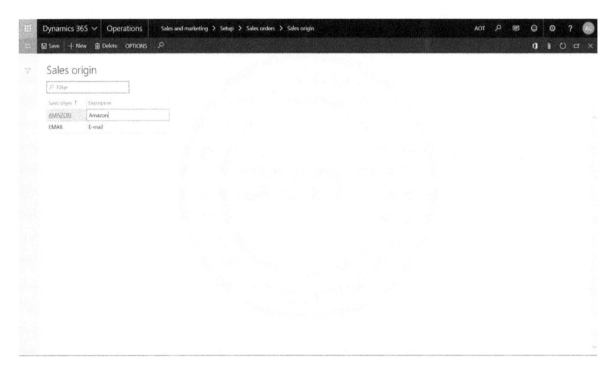

Step 2: Update the Sales origin and update the Description

Then we will be able to add a code and description to our new record.

To do this we will just need to update the **Sales origin** value and change the **Description** value.

This time, we will want to set the **Sales origin** to **AMAZON** and set the **Description** to **Amazon**.

dync
www.dynamicscompanions.com
Dynamics Companions

- 134 -

www.blindsquirrelpublishing.com
© 2019 Blind Squirrel Publishing, LLC , All Rights Reserved

BLIND SQUIRREL
PUBLISHING

DYNAMICS COMPANIONS
BARE BONES CONFIGURATION GUIDE

CONFIGURING SALES ORDER MANAGEMENT WITHIN DYNAMICS 365 FOR FINANCE & OPERATIONS
MODULE 1: CONFIGURING SALES ORDER MANAGEMENT CONTROLS

Creating an Trade Show Sales origin code

Let's continue on and create some more possible channels for our sales orders, and create one for Trade shows.

How to do it...

Step 1: Click on the New button, update the Sales origin and update the Description

We can create a new record for trade show leads just the same way as we created the other records.

Click on the **New** button, set the **Sales origin** to **TRADESHOW** and change the **Description** to **Trade Show**.

dync

www.dynamicscompanions.com
Dynamics Companions

- 135 -

www.blindsquirrelpublishing.com
© 2019 Blind Squirrel Publishing, LLC , All Rights Reserved

BLIND SQUIRREL
PUBLISHING

DYNAMICS COMPANIONS
BARE BONES CONFIGURATION GUIDE

CONFIGURING SALES ORDER MANAGEMENT WITHIN DYNAMICS 365 FOR FINANCE & OPERATIONS
MODULE 1: CONFIGURING SALES ORDER MANAGEMENT CONTROLS

Creating an Trade Show Sales origin code

How to do it...

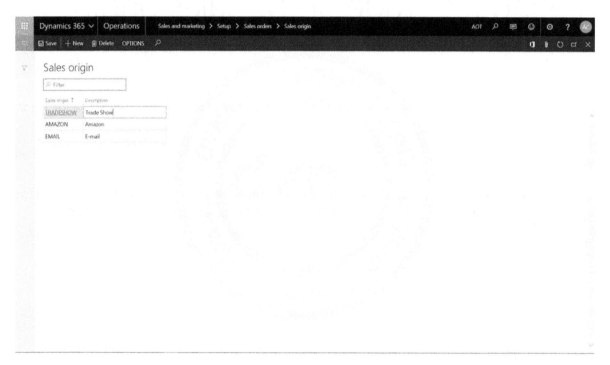

Step 1: Click on the New button, update the Sales origin and update the Description

We can create a new record for trade show leads just the same way as we created the other records.

To do this all we need to do is click on the **New** button in the menu bar, update the **Sales origin** value and update the **Description** value.

This time, we will want to set the **Sales origin** to **TRADESHOW** and set the **Description** to **Trade Show**.

dync
www.dynamicscompanions.com
Dynamics Companions

- 136 -

www.blindsquirrelpublishing.com
© 2019 Blind Squirrel Publishing, LLC , All Rights Reserved

BLIND SQUIRREL
PUBLISHING

DYNAMICS COMPANIONS
BARE BONES CONFIGURATION GUIDE

CONFIGURING SALES ORDER MANAGEMENT WITHIN DYNAMICS 365 FOR FINANCE & OPERATIONS
MODULE 1: CONFIGURING SALES ORDER MANAGEMENT CONTROLS

Creating an Phone Sales origin code

Next we will add the option to have leads acquired through phone inquiries.

How to do it...

Step 1: Click on the New button, update the Sales origin and update the Description

We can create a new record for phone call orders.

Click on the **New** button, change the **Sales origin** to **PHONE** and change the **Description** to **Phone**.

www.dynamicscompanions.com
Dynamics Companions

- 137 -

www.blindsquirrelpublishing.com
© 2019 Blind Squirrel Publishing, LLC, All Rights Reserved

BLIND SQUIRREL
PUBLISHING

DYNAMICS COMPANIONS
BARE BONES CONFIGURATION GUIDE

CONFIGURING SALES ORDER MANAGEMENT WITHIN DYNAMICS 365 FOR FINANCE & OPERATIONS
MODULE 1: CONFIGURING SALES ORDER MANAGEMENT CONTROLS

Creating an Phone Sales origin code

How to do it...

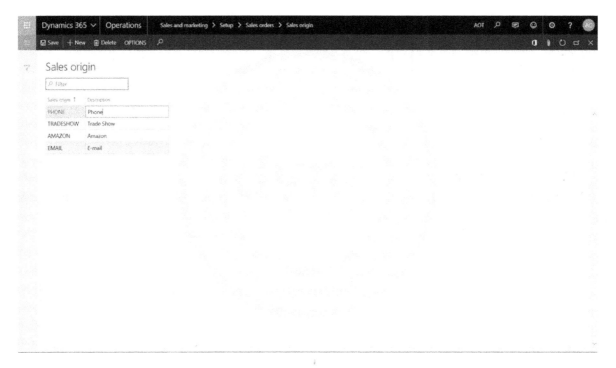

Step 1: Click on the New button, update the Sales origin and update the Description

We can create a new record for phone call orders.

To do this just click on the **New** button in the menu bar, update the **Sales origin** value and update the **Description** value.

For this example, we will want to set the **Sales origin** to **PHONE** and set the **Description** to **Phone**.

dyn c
www.dynamicscompanions.com
Dynamics Companions

- 138 -

www.blindsquirrelpublishing.com
© 2019 Blind Squirrel Publishing, LLC, All Rights Reserved

BLIND SQUIRREL
PUBLISHING

DYNAMICS COMPANIONS
BARE BONES CONFIGURATION GUIDE

CONFIGURING SALES ORDER MANAGEMENT WITHIN DYNAMICS 365 FOR FINANCE & OPERATIONS
MODULE 1: CONFIGURING SALES ORDER MANAGEMENT CONTROLS

Creating an Mail Sales origin code

We are still a little old fashioned, so we will add another Sales origin code for orders that come in thought the mail.

How to do it...

Step 1: Click on the New button, update the Sales origin and update the Description

Let's add another record like we did before for the mail option.

Click on the **New** button, change the **Sales origin** to **MAIL** and set the **Description** to **Mail**.

dyn c
www.dynamicscompanions.com
Dynamics Companions

- 139 -

www.blindsquirrelpublishing.com
© 2019 Blind Squirrel Publishing, LLC, All Rights Reserved

BLIND SQUIRREL
PUBLISHING

DYNAMICS COMPANIONS
BARE BONES CONFIGURATION GUIDE

CONFIGURING SALES ORDER MANAGEMENT WITHIN DYNAMICS 365 FOR FINANCE & OPERATIONS
MODULE 1: CONFIGURING SALES ORDER MANAGEMENT CONTROLS

Creating an Mail Sales origin code

How to do it...

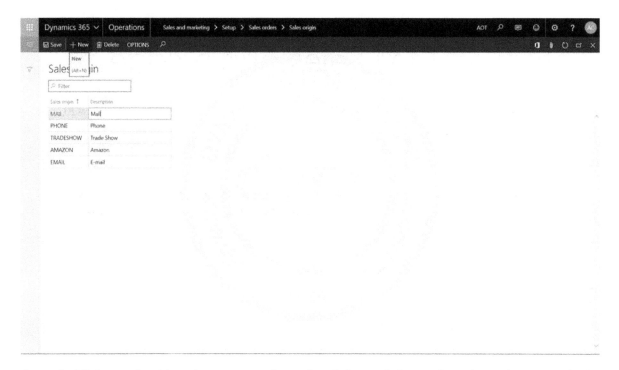

Step 1: Click on the New button, update the Sales origin and update the Description

Let's add another record like we did before for the mail option.

To do this just click on the **New** button in the menu bar, change the **Sales origin** value and change the **Description** value.

This time, we will want to set the **Sales origin** to **MAIL** and set the **Description** to **Mail**.

www.dynamicscompanions.com
Dynamics Companions

- 140 -

www.blindsquirrelpublishing.com
© 2019 Blind Squirrel Publishing, LLC , All Rights Reserved

BLIND SQUIRREL
PUBLISHING

DYNAMICS COMPANIONS
BARE BONES CONFIGURATION GUIDE

CONFIGURING SALES ORDER MANAGEMENT WITHIN DYNAMICS 365 FOR FINANCE & OPERATIONS
MODULE 1: CONFIGURING SALES ORDER MANAGEMENT CONTROLS

Creating an Website Sales origin code

If we have an ecommerce channel within the business then we might also want to track all of the orders that originate through the website.

How to do it...

Step 1: Click on the New button, update the Sales origin and update the Description

By now you should know the process of creating the website origin code, but just in case here we go.

Click on the **New** button, change the **Sales origin** to **WEBSITE** and set the **Description** to **Website**.

dync
www.dynamicscompanions.com
Dynamics Companions

www.blindsquirrelpublishing.com
© 2019 Blind Squirrel Publishing, LLC, All Rights Reserved

BLIND SQUIRREL
PUBLISHING

DYNAMICS COMPANIONS
BARE BONES CONFIGURATION GUIDE

CONFIGURING SALES ORDER MANAGEMENT WITHIN DYNAMICS 365 FOR FINANCE & OPERATIONS
MODULE 1: CONFIGURING SALES ORDER MANAGEMENT CONTROLS

Creating an Website Sales origin code

How to do it...

Step 1: Click on the New button, update the Sales origin and update the Description

By now you should know the process of creating the website origin code, but just in case here we go.

To do this all we need to do is click on the **New** button in the menu bar, change the **Sales origin** value and change the **Description** value.

This time, we will want to set the **Sales origin** to **WEBSITE** and set the **Description** to **Website**.

dync
www.dynamicscompanions.com
Dynamics Companions

- 142 -

www.blindsquirrelpublishing.com
© 2019 Blind Squirrel Publishing, LLC, All Rights Reserved

BLIND SQUIRREL
PUBLISHING

DYNAMICS COMPANIONS
BARE BONES CONFIGURATION GUIDE

CONFIGURING SALES ORDER MANAGEMENT WITHIN DYNAMICS 365 FOR FINANCE & OPERATIONS
MODULE 1: CONFIGURING SALES ORDER MANAGEMENT CONTROLS

Creating an Fax Sales origin code

And finally we will add one more Sales origin code for all of those customers trapped in the 90's that still send their orders through as a Fax.

How to do it...

Step 1: Click on the New button, update the Sales origin and update the Description

Click on the **New** button, change the **Sales origin** to **FAX** and change the **Description** to **Fax**.

DYNAMICS COMPANIONS
BARE BONES CONFIGURATION GUIDE

CONFIGURING SALES ORDER MANAGEMENT WITHIN DYNAMICS 365 FOR FINANCE & OPERATIONS
MODULE 1: CONFIGURING SALES ORDER MANAGEMENT CONTROLS

Creating an Fax Sales origin code

How to do it...

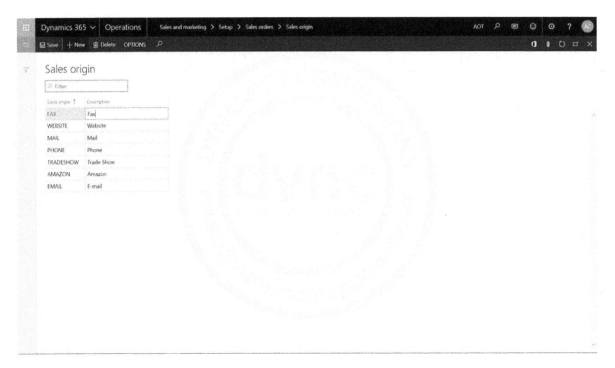

Step 1: Click on the New button, update the Sales origin and update the Description

To do this just click on the **New** button in the menu bar, update the **Sales origin** value and change the **Description** value.

This time, we will want to set the **Sales origin** to **FAX** and set the **Description** to **Fax**.

dyn c
www.dynamicscompanions.com
Dynamics Companions

- 144 -

www.blindsquirrelpublishing.com
© 2019 Blind Squirrel Publishing, LLC , All Rights Reserved

BLIND SQUIRREL
PUBLISHING

DYNAMICS COMPANIONS
BARE BONES CONFIGURATION GUIDE

CONFIGURING SALES ORDER MANAGEMENT WITHIN DYNAMICS 365 FOR FINANCE & OPERATIONS
MODULE 1: CONFIGURING SALES ORDER MANAGEMENT CONTROLS

Creating an Fax Sales origin code

How to do it...

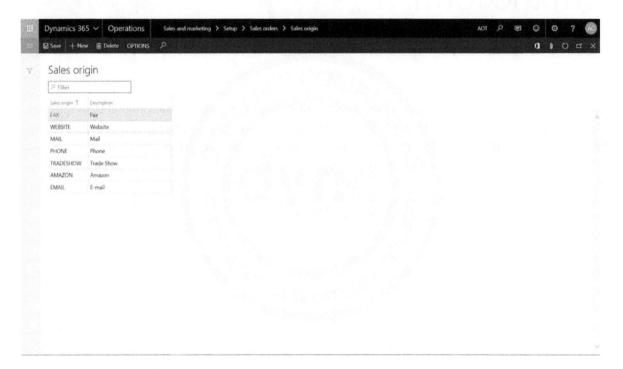

Step 1: Click on the New button, update the Sales origin and update the Description

After we have done that we can just exit from the form.

www.dynamicscompanions.com
Dynamics Companions

- 145 -

www.blindsquirrelpublishing.com
© 2019 Blind Squirrel Publishing, LLC , All Rights Reserved

BLIND SQUIRREL
PUBLISHING

DYNAMICS COMPANIONS
BARE BONES CONFIGURATION GUIDE

CONFIGURING SALES ORDER MANAGEMENT WITHIN DYNAMICS 365 FOR FINANCE & OPERATIONS
MODULE 1: CONFIGURING SALES ORDER MANAGEMENT CONTROLS

After we have done that we can just exit from the form.

Congratulations. Now we have a way to categorize all of our sales orders and the original sales channel that they were created through. This will help us later on when we create sales reports against the orders to see what order originating point is the most useful in generating sales.

DYNAMICS COMPANIONS
BARE BONES CONFIGURATION GUIDE

CONFIGURING SALES ORDER MANAGEMENT WITHIN DYNAMICS 365 FOR FINANCE & OPERATIONS
MODULE 1: CONFIGURING SALES ORDER MANAGEMENT CONTROLS

Enabling Order Event Tracking

Now we will turn on a few features related to order management, starting with the **Order Event Tracking** which will allow you to see all of the changed that are made to Sales Orders.

Topics Covered

- Opening the Order Events configuration form

- Enabling Order events

- Review

dync
www.dynamicscompanions.com
Dynamics Companions

- 147 -

www.blindsquirrelpublishing.com
© 2019 Blind Squirrel Publishing, LLC, All Rights Reserved

BLIND SQUIRREL
PUBLISHING

DYNAMICS COMPANIONS
BARE BONES CONFIGURATION GUIDE

CONFIGURING SALES ORDER MANAGEMENT WITHIN DYNAMICS 365 FOR FINANCE & OPERATIONS
MODULE 1: CONFIGURING SALES ORDER MANAGEMENT CONTROLS

Opening the Order Events configuration form

We will want to start off by opening up the form that we will use to configure the event options within the order management functions.

How to do it...

Step 1: Open the Order events form through the menu

We can get to the **Order events** form a couple of different ways. The first way is through the master menu.

Navigate to Sales and marketing > Setup > Events > Order events.

Step 2: Open the Order events form through the menu search

Another way that we can find the **Order events** form is through the menu search feature.

Type in **order eve** into the menu search and select **Order events**.

www.dynamicscompanions.com
Dynamics Companions

- 148 -

www.blindsquirrelpublishing.com
© 2019 Blind Squirrel Publishing, LLC , All Rights Reserved

BLIND SQUIRREL
PUBLISHING

DYNAMICS COMPANIONS
BARE BONES CONFIGURATION GUIDE

CONFIGURING SALES ORDER MANAGEMENT WITHIN DYNAMICS 365 FOR FINANCE & OPERATIONS
MODULE 1: CONFIGURING SALES ORDER MANAGEMENT CONTROLS

Opening the Order Events configuration form

How to do it...

Step 1: Open the Order events form through the menu

We can get to the **Order events** form a couple of different ways. The first way is through the master menu.

To do this, open up the navigation panel, expand out the **Modules** and group, and click on **Sales and marketing** to see all of the menu items that are available. Then click on the **Order events** menu item within the **Events** folder of the **Setup** group.

dync

www.dynamicscompanions.com
Dynamics Companions

- 149 -

www.blindsquirrelpublishing.com
© 2019 Blind Squirrel Publishing, LLC , All Rights Reserved

BLIND SQUIRREL
PUBLISHING

DYNAMICS COMPANIONS
BARE BONES CONFIGURATION GUIDE

CONFIGURING SALES ORDER MANAGEMENT WITHIN DYNAMICS 365 FOR FINANCE & OPERATIONS
MODULE 1: CONFIGURING SALES ORDER MANAGEMENT CONTROLS

Opening the Order Events configuration form

How to do it...

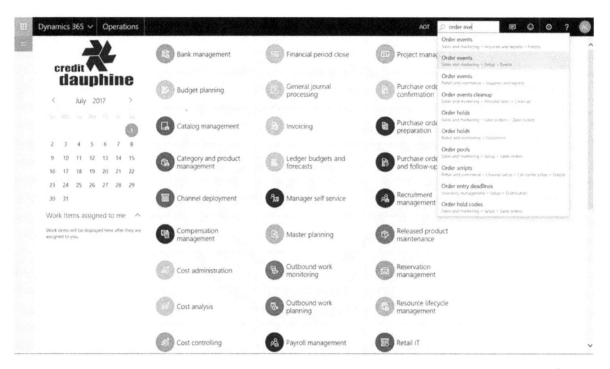

Step 2: Open the Order events form through the menu search

Another way that we can find the **Order events** form is through the menu search feature.

We can do this by clicking on the search icon in the header of the form (or by pressing **ALT+G**) and then type in **order eve** into the search box. Then you will be able to select the **Order events** form from the dropdown list.

dync
www.dynamicscompanions.com
Dynamics Companions

- 150 -

www.blindsquirrelpublishing.com
© 2019 Blind Squirrel Publishing, LLC , All Rights Reserved

BLIND SQUIRREL
PUBLISHING

DYNAMICS COMPANIONS
BARE BONES CONFIGURATION GUIDE

CONFIGURING SALES ORDER MANAGEMENT WITHIN DYNAMICS 365 FOR FINANCE & OPERATIONS
MODULE 1: CONFIGURING SALES ORDER MANAGEMENT CONTROLS

Opening the Order Events configuration form

How to do it...

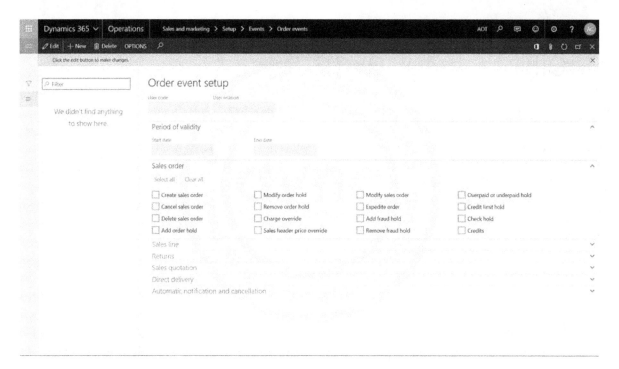

Step 2: Open the Order events form through the menu search

This will open up the **Order event setup** maintenance form is displayed and we will be able to see all of the different events that you can track.

www.dynamicscompanions.com
Dynamics Companions

- 151 -

www.blindsquirrelpublishing.com
© 2019 Blind Squirrel Publishing, LLC, All Rights Reserved

BLIND SQUIRREL
PUBLISHING

DYNAMICS COMPANIONS
BARE BONES CONFIGURATION GUIDE

CONFIGURING SALES ORDER MANAGEMENT WITHIN DYNAMICS 365 FOR FINANCE & OPERATIONS
MODULE 1: CONFIGURING SALES ORDER MANAGEMENT CONTROLS

Enabling Order events

Now we can set up the order events to track changes to a number of different events.

How to do it...

Step 1: Click on the New button

Let's start off by creating an event record that we will use to identify what will be creating the events and also what events we will be notified about.

Click on the **New** button.

Step 2: Choose the User code

We will want to apply these events to track all order changes regardless of the user that made the change.

Click on the **User code** dropdown list And select **All**.

Step 3: Click on the Select all button

We will start off by selecting the events that we want to track on the Sales order.

Although you can track individual event types, it is simpler just to select all of the different event types within the Sales order fast tab.

Click on the **Select all** button.

Step 4: Expand Sales line tab

Now we will want to look at the events that we can track on the sales order lines.

Expand the **Sales line** tab.

Step 5: Click on the Select all button

We will just select all of the events here as well so that we can see all of the changes that are mode on the sales order lines.

Click on the **Select all** button.

Step 6: Expand Returns tab

Finally we will look at the different events that we can track on the sales order returns.

Expand the **Returns** tab.

Step 7: Click on the Select all button

We want to be fully informed of changes that are made on the sales returns as well so we will select all of the event options.

Click on the **Select all** button.

DYNAMICS COMPANIONS
BARE BONES CONFIGURATION GUIDE

CONFIGURING SALES ORDER MANAGEMENT WITHIN DYNAMICS 365 FOR FINANCE & OPERATIONS
MODULE 1: CONFIGURING SALES ORDER MANAGEMENT CONTROLS

Enabling Order events

How to do it...

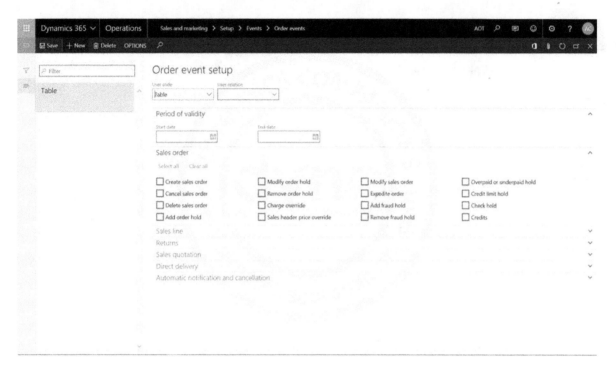

Step 1: Click on the New button

Let's start off by creating an event record that we will use to identify what will be creating the events and also what events we will be notified about.

To do this all we need to do is click on the **New** button in the menu bar.

www.dynamicscompanions.com
Dynamics Companions

- 153 -

www.blindsquirrelpublishing.com
© 2019 Blind Squirrel Publishing, LLC, All Rights Reserved

BLIND SQUIRREL
PUBLISHING

DYNAMICS COMPANIONS
BARE BONES CONFIGURATION GUIDE

CONFIGURING SALES ORDER MANAGEMENT WITHIN DYNAMICS 365 FOR FINANCE & OPERATIONS
MODULE 1: CONFIGURING SALES ORDER MANAGEMENT CONTROLS

Enabling Order events

How to do it...

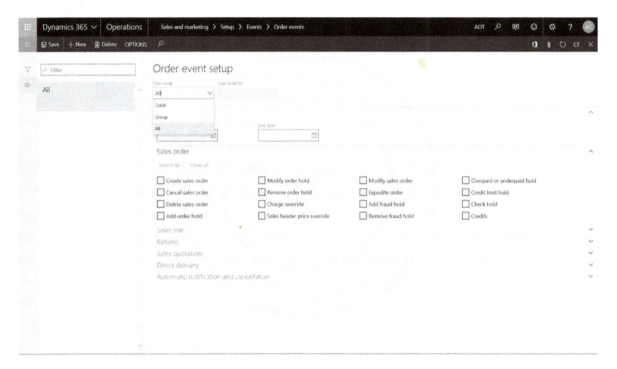

Step 2: Choose the User code

We will want to apply these events to track all order changes regardless of the user that made the change.

To do this we will just need to select the **User code** option from the dropdown list.

For this example, we will want to click on the **User code** dropdown list and select **All**.

DYNAMICS COMPANIONS
BARE BONES CONFIGURATION GUIDE

CONFIGURING SALES ORDER MANAGEMENT WITHIN DYNAMICS 365 FOR FINANCE & OPERATIONS
MODULE 1: CONFIGURING SALES ORDER MANAGEMENT CONTROLS

Enabling Order events

How to do it...

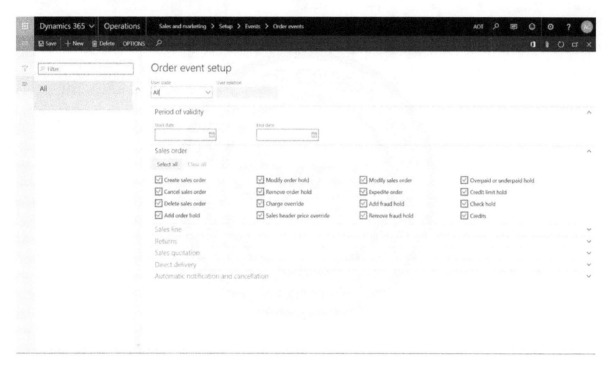

Step 3: Click on the Select all button

We will start off by selecting the events that we want to track on the Sales order.

Although you can track individual event types, it is simpler just to select all of the different event types within the Sales order fast tab.

To do this just click on the **Select all** button.

dync

www.dynamicscompanions.com
Dynamics Companions

- 155 -

www.blindsquirrelpublishing.com
© 2019 Blind Squirrel Publishing, LLC , All Rights Reserved

BLIND SQUIRREL
PUBLISHING

DYNAMICS COMPANIONS
BARE BONES CONFIGURATION GUIDE

CONFIGURING SALES ORDER MANAGEMENT WITHIN DYNAMICS 365 FOR FINANCE & OPERATIONS
MODULE 1: CONFIGURING SALES ORDER MANAGEMENT CONTROLS

Enabling Order events

How to do it...

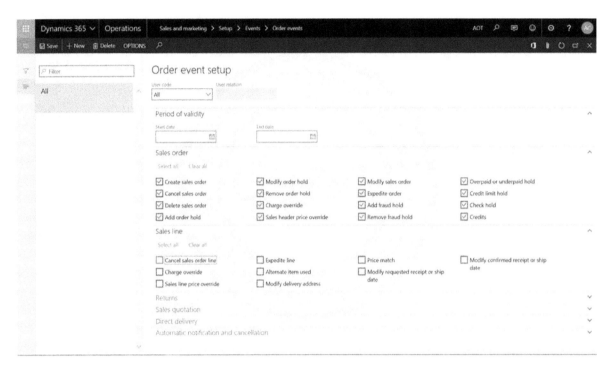

Step 4: Expand Sales line tab

Now we will want to look at the events that we can track on the sales order lines.

To do this all we need to do is expand the **Sales line** tab.

www.dynamicscompanions.com
Dynamics Companions

- 156 -

www.blindsquirrelpublishing.com
© 2019 Blind Squirrel Publishing, LLC , All Rights Reserved

BLIND SQUIRREL
PUBLISHING

DYNAMICS COMPANIONS
BARE BONES CONFIGURATION GUIDE

CONFIGURING SALES ORDER MANAGEMENT WITHIN DYNAMICS 365 FOR FINANCE & OPERATIONS
MODULE 1: CONFIGURING SALES ORDER MANAGEMENT CONTROLS

Enabling Order events

How to do it...

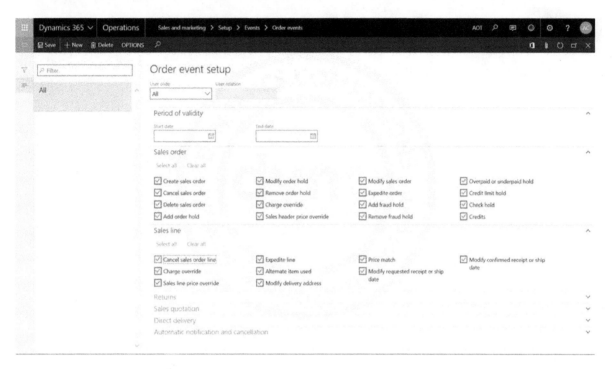

Step 5: Click on the Select all button

We will just select all of the events here as well so that we can see all of the changes that are mode on the sales order lines.

To do this all we need to do is click on the **Select all** button.

dync
www.dynamicscompanions.com
Dynamics Companions

- 157 -

www.blindsquirrelpublishing.com
© 2019 Blind Squirrel Publishing, LLC, All Rights Reserved

BLIND SQUIRREL
PUBLISHING

DYNAMICS COMPANIONS
BARE BONES CONFIGURATION GUIDE

CONFIGURING SALES ORDER MANAGEMENT WITHIN DYNAMICS 365 FOR FINANCE & OPERATIONS
MODULE 1: CONFIGURING SALES ORDER MANAGEMENT CONTROLS

Enabling Order events

How to do it...

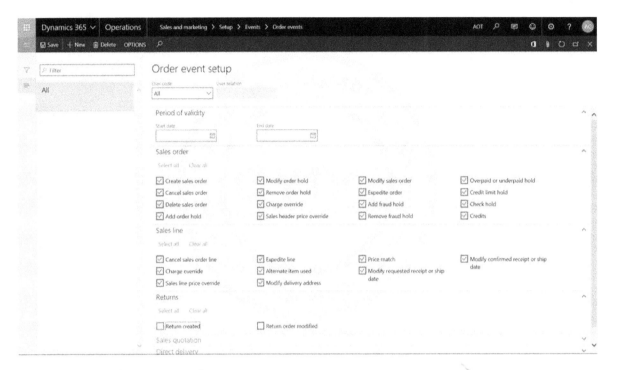

Step 6: Expand Returns tab

Finally we will look at the different events that we can track on the sales order returns.

To do this all we need to do is expand the **Returns** tab.

dyn c
dynamics companions

www.dynamicscompanions.com
Dynamics Companions

- 158 -

www.blindsquirrelpublishing.com
© 2019 Blind Squirrel Publishing, LLC , All Rights Reserved

BLIND SQUIRREL
PUBLISHING

DYNAMICS COMPANIONS
BARE BONES CONFIGURATION GUIDE

CONFIGURING SALES ORDER MANAGEMENT WITHIN DYNAMICS 365 FOR FINANCE & OPERATIONS
MODULE 1: CONFIGURING SALES ORDER MANAGEMENT CONTROLS

Enabling Order events

How to do it...

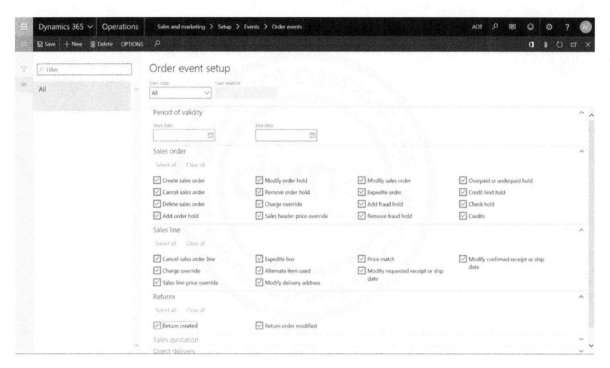

Step 7: Click on the Select all button

We want to be fully informed of changes that are made on the sales returns as well so we will select all of the event options.

To do this all we need to do is click on the **Select all** button.

When you have done that, just exit from the form.

dyn c

www.dynamicscompanions.com
Dynamics Companions

- 159 -

www.blindsquirrelpublishing.com
© 2019 Blind Squirrel Publishing, LLC , All Rights Reserved

BLIND SQUIRREL
PUBLISHING

DYNAMICS COMPANIONS
BARE BONES CONFIGURATION GUIDE

CONFIGURING SALES ORDER MANAGEMENT WITHIN DYNAMICS 365 FOR FINANCE & OPERATIONS
MODULE 1: CONFIGURING SALES ORDER MANAGEMENT CONTROLS

Review

How easy was that. We have now enabled a whole lot of different options that will allow us to track changes against our sales orders when we start maintaining them and modifying them.

DYNAMICS COMPANIONS
BARE BONES CONFIGURATION GUIDE

CONFIGURING SALES ORDER MANAGEMENT WITHIN DYNAMICS 365 FOR FINANCE & OPERATIONS
MODULE 1: CONFIGURING SALES ORDER MANAGEMENT CONTROLS

Configuring Order Search Parameters

Another very useful feature to enable within Order Management is the **Order Search**. This will allow you to search on multiple fields within the Products and Customers at the time of order entry, and it will return back either the only matching record, or a list of records that match. Before we configure how the search works, we just want to enable it.

Topics Covered

- Opening the Search Parameters options form

- Configuring the Search parameters

- Review

- Opening up the Search criteria maintenance form

- Configuring the Customer search criteria

- Configuring the Product search criteria

- Review

dync
www.dynamicscompanions.com
Dynamics Companions

- 161 -

www.blindsquirrelpublishing.com
© 2019 Blind Squirrel Publishing, LLC , All Rights Reserved

BLIND SQUIRREL
PUBLISHING

DYNAMICS COMPANIONS
BARE BONES CONFIGURATION GUIDE

CONFIGURING SALES ORDER MANAGEMENT WITHIN DYNAMICS 365 FOR FINANCE & OPERATIONS
MODULE 1: CONFIGURING SALES ORDER MANAGEMENT CONTROLS

Opening the Search Parameters options form

To do this we will need to use the **Search parameters** form to set up this feature.

How to do it...

Step 1: Open the Search parameters form through the menu

We can get to the **Search parameters** form a couple of different ways. The first way is through the master menu.

Navigate to Sales and Marketing > Setup > Search > Search parameters.

Step 2: Open the Search parameters form through the menu search

Another way that we can find the **Search parameters** form is through the menu search feature.

Type in **search pa** into the menu search and select **Search parameters**.

dyn c
www.dynamicscompanions.com
Dynamics Companions

- 162 -

www.blindsquirrelpublishing.com
© 2019 Blind Squirrel Publishing, LLC , All Rights Reserved

BLIND SQUIRREL
PUBLISHING

DYNAMICS COMPANIONS
BARE BONES CONFIGURATION GUIDE

CONFIGURING SALES ORDER MANAGEMENT WITHIN DYNAMICS 365 FOR FINANCE & OPERATIONS
MODULE 1: CONFIGURING SALES ORDER MANAGEMENT CONTROLS

Opening the Search Parameters options form

How to do it...

Step 1: Open the Search parameters form through the menu

We can get to the **Search parameters** form a couple of different ways. The first way is through the master menu.

In order to do this, open up the navigation panel, expand out the **Modules** and group, and click on **Sales and Marketing** to see all of the menu items that are available. Then click on the **Search parameters** menu item within the **Search** folder of the **Setup** group.

dyn c
www.dynamicscompanions.com
Dynamics Companions

- 163 -

www.blindsquirrelpublishing.com
© 2019 Blind Squirrel Publishing, LLC , All Rights Reserved

BLIND SQUIRREL
PUBLISHING

DYNAMICS COMPANIONS
BARE BONES CONFIGURATION GUIDE

CONFIGURING SALES ORDER MANAGEMENT WITHIN DYNAMICS 365 FOR FINANCE & OPERATIONS
MODULE 1: CONFIGURING SALES ORDER MANAGEMENT CONTROLS

Opening the Search Parameters options form

How to do it...

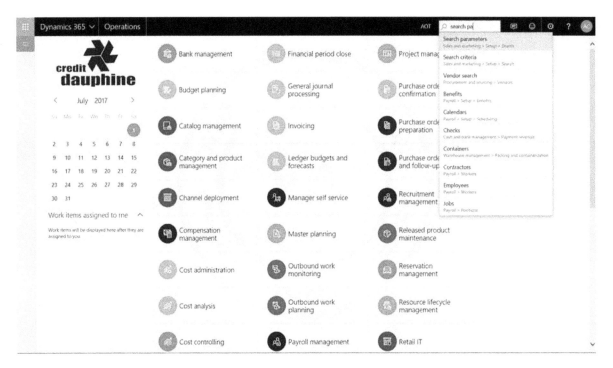

Step 2: Open the Search parameters form through the menu search

Another way that we can find the **Search parameters** form is through the menu search feature.

We can do this by clicking on the search icon in the header of the form (or by pressing **ALT+G**) and then type in **search pa** into the search box. Then you will be able to select the **Search parameters** form from the dropdown list.

dyn c
www.dynamicscompanions.com
Dynamics Companions

- 164 -

www.blindsquirrelpublishing.com
© 2019 Blind Squirrel Publishing, LLC , All Rights Reserved

BLIND SQUIRREL
PUBLISHING

DYNAMICS COMPANIONS
BARE BONES CONFIGURATION GUIDE

CONFIGURING SALES ORDER MANAGEMENT WITHIN DYNAMICS 365 FOR FINANCE & OPERATIONS
MODULE 1: CONFIGURING SALES ORDER MANAGEMENT CONTROLS

Opening the Search Parameters options form

How to do it...

Step 2: Open the Search parameters form through the menu search

This will open up the **Search Parameters** dialog box.

dync
www.dynamicscompanions.com
Dynamics Companions

- 165 -

www.blindsquirrelpublishing.com
© 2019 Blind Squirrel Publishing, LLC , All Rights Reserved

BLIND SQUIRREL
PUBLISHING

DYNAMICS COMPANIONS
BARE BONES CONFIGURATION GUIDE

CONFIGURING SALES ORDER MANAGEMENT WITHIN DYNAMICS 365 FOR FINANCE & OPERATIONS
MODULE 1: CONFIGURING SALES ORDER MANAGEMENT CONTROLS

Configuring the Search parameters

Now we can set up the options that will allow us to search for products as we are creating sales orders.

How to do it...

Step 1: Change the Automatically fill customer search

The first option that we will turn on will be the option to search for customers based off key fields.

Toggle the Automatically fill customer search switch And set it to Yes.

Step 2: Toggle the Automatically fill item search

The next option that we will want to enable will be the one that will search for products as we are creating the orders based of key fields.

Change the **Automatically fill item search** switch And set it to **Yes**.

Step 3: Toggle the Enable lookup for product search

Next we will want to enable the option that will allow us to use the lookup for the product search.

Change the Enable lookup for product search switch And set it to Yes.

Step 4: Toggle the Save search type

And finally, to finish things off we will allow the system to save out search options.

Change the **Save search type** switch And set it to **Yes**.

www.dynamicscompanions.com
Dynamics Companions

- 166 -

www.blindsquirrelpublishing.com
© 2019 Blind Squirrel Publishing, LLC , All Rights Reserved

BLIND SQUIRREL
PUBLISHING

DYNAMICS COMPANIONS
BARE BONES CONFIGURATION GUIDE

CONFIGURING SALES ORDER MANAGEMENT WITHIN DYNAMICS 365 FOR FINANCE & OPERATIONS
MODULE 1: CONFIGURING SALES ORDER MANAGEMENT CONTROLS

Configuring the Search parameters

How to do it...

Step 1: Change the Automatically fill customer search

The first option that we will turn on will be the option to search for customers based off key fields.

To do this just switch the **Automatically fill customer search** value.

This time, we will want to click on the **Automatically fill customer search** toggle switch and set it to the **Yes** value.

www.dynamicscompanions.com
Dynamics Companions

- 167 -

www.blindsquirrelpublishing.com
© 2019 Blind Squirrel Publishing, LLC , All Rights Reserved

BLIND SQUIRREL
PUBLISHING

DYNAMICS COMPANIONS
BARE BONES CONFIGURATION GUIDE

CONFIGURING SALES ORDER MANAGEMENT WITHIN DYNAMICS 365 FOR FINANCE & OPERATIONS
MODULE 1: CONFIGURING SALES ORDER MANAGEMENT CONTROLS

Configuring the Search parameters

How to do it...

Step 2: Toggle the Automatically fill item search

The next option that we will want to enable will be the one that will search for products as we are creating the orders based of key fields.

To do this we will just need to switch the **Automatically fill item search** value.

For this example, we will want to click on the **Automatically fill item search** toggle switch and update it to the **Yes** value.

BLIND SQUIRREL
PUBLISHING

DYNAMICS COMPANIONS
BARE BONES CONFIGURATION GUIDE

CONFIGURING SALES ORDER MANAGEMENT WITHIN DYNAMICS 365 FOR FINANCE & OPERATIONS
MODULE 1: CONFIGURING SALES ORDER MANAGEMENT CONTROLS

Configuring the Search parameters

How to do it...

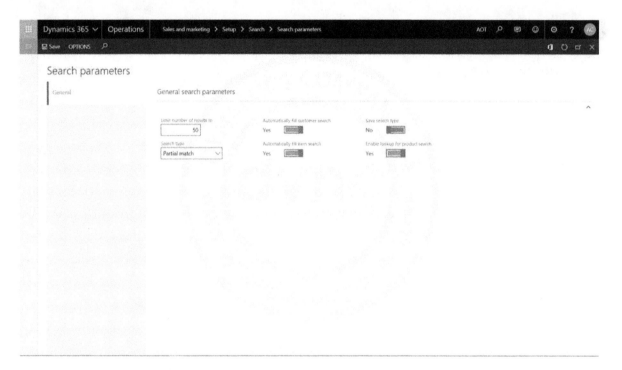

Step 3: Toggle the Enable lookup for product search

Next we will want to enable the option that will allow us to use the lookup for the product search.

To do this we will just need to toggle the **Enable lookup for product search** option.

This time, we will want to click on the **Enable lookup for product search** toggle switch and update it to the **Yes** value.

www.dynamicscompanions.com
Dynamics Companions

- 169 -

www.blindsquirrelpublishing.com
© 2019 Blind Squirrel Publishing, LLC , All Rights Reserved

BLIND SQUIRREL
PUBLISHING

DYNAMICS COMPANIONS
BARE BONES CONFIGURATION GUIDE

CONFIGURING SALES ORDER MANAGEMENT WITHIN DYNAMICS 365 FOR FINANCE & OPERATIONS
MODULE 1: CONFIGURING SALES ORDER MANAGEMENT CONTROLS

Configuring the Search parameters

How to do it...

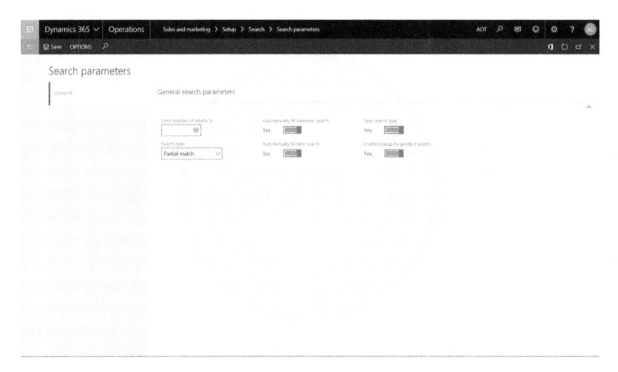

Step 4: Toggle the Save search type

And finally, to finish things off we will allow the system to save out search options.

To do this we will just need to switch the **Save search type** option.

For this example, we will want to click on the **Save search type** toggle switch and change it to the **Yes** value.

www.dynamicscompanions.com
Dynamics Companions

- 170 -

www.blindsquirrelpublishing.com
© 2019 Blind Squirrel Publishing, LLC , All Rights Reserved

BLIND SQUIRREL
PUBLISHING

DYNAMICS COMPANIONS
BARE BONES CONFIGURATION GUIDE

CONFIGURING SALES ORDER MANAGEMENT WITHIN DYNAMICS 365 FOR FINANCE & OPERATIONS
MODULE 1: CONFIGURING SALES ORDER MANAGEMENT CONTROLS

Review

DYNAMICS COMPANIONS
BARE BONES CONFIGURATION GUIDE

CONFIGURING SALES ORDER MANAGEMENT WITHIN DYNAMICS 365 FOR FINANCE & OPERATIONS
MODULE 1: CONFIGURING SALES ORDER MANAGEMENT CONTROLS

Opening up the Search criteria maintenance form

To do this we will need to set up the search criteria that we will want to use, and to do that we will want to open up the Search criteria maintenance form.

How to do it...

Step 1: Open the Search criteria form through the menu

We can get to the **Search criteria** form a couple of different ways. The first way is through the master menu.

Navigate to Sales and marketing > Setup > Search > Search criteria.

Step 2: Open the Search criteria form through the menu search

Another way that we can find the **Search criteria** form is through the menu search feature.

Type in **search cri** into the menu search and select **Search criteria**.

DYNAMICS COMPANIONS
BARE BONES CONFIGURATION GUIDE

CONFIGURING SALES ORDER MANAGEMENT WITHIN DYNAMICS 365 FOR FINANCE & OPERATIONS
MODULE 1: CONFIGURING SALES ORDER MANAGEMENT CONTROLS

Opening up the Search criteria maintenance form

How to do it...

Step 1: Open the Search criteria form through the menu

We can get to the **Search criteria** form a couple of different ways. The first way is through the master menu.

In order to do this, open up the navigation panel, expand out the **Modules** and group, and click on **Sales and marketing** to see all of the menu items that are available. Then click on the **Search criteria** menu item within the **Search** folder of the **Setup** group.

DYNAMICS COMPANIONS
BARE BONES CONFIGURATION GUIDE

CONFIGURING SALES ORDER MANAGEMENT WITHIN DYNAMICS 365 FOR FINANCE & OPERATIONS
MODULE 1: CONFIGURING SALES ORDER MANAGEMENT CONTROLS

Opening up the Search criteria maintenance form

How to do it...

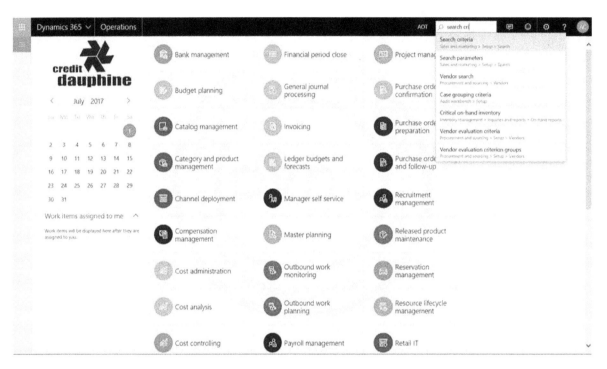

Step 2: Open the Search criteria form through the menu search

Another way that we can find the **Search criteria** form is through the menu search feature.

We can do this by clicking on the search icon in the header of the form (or by pressing **ALT+G**) and then type in **search cri** into the search box. Then you will be able to select the **Search criteria** form from the dropdown list.

dyn c
Dynamics Companions

www.dynamicscompanions.com
Dynamics Companions

- 174 -

www.blindsquirrelpublishing.com
© 2019 Blind Squirrel Publishing, LLC, All Rights Reserved

BLIND SQUIRREL
PUBLISHING

DYNAMICS COMPANIONS
BARE BONES CONFIGURATION GUIDE

CONFIGURING SALES ORDER MANAGEMENT WITHIN DYNAMICS 365 FOR FINANCE & OPERATIONS
MODULE 1: CONFIGURING SALES ORDER MANAGEMENT CONTROLS

Opening up the Search criteria maintenance form

How to do it...

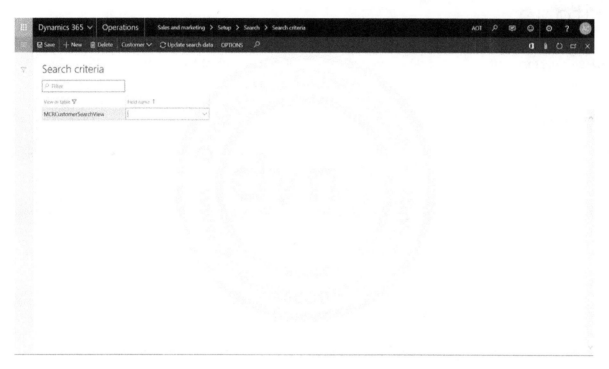

Step 2: Open the Search criteria form through the menu search

This will open up the **Search criteria** maintenance form where we can set up all of the fields that we will want to be able to search for customers and products by.

www.dynamicscompanions.com
Dynamics Companions

- 175 -

www.blindsquirrelpublishing.com
© 2019 Blind Squirrel Publishing, LLC , All Rights Reserved

BLIND SQUIRREL
PUBLISHING

DYNAMICS COMPANIONS
BARE BONES CONFIGURATION GUIDE

CONFIGURING SALES ORDER MANAGEMENT WITHIN DYNAMICS 365 FOR FINANCE & OPERATIONS
MODULE 1: CONFIGURING SALES ORDER MANAGEMENT CONTROLS

Configuring the Customer search criteria

Now we can start configuring the search options and fields that we want to search within the sales orders for. We will start off by configuring the customer search criteria.

How to do it...

Step 1: Click on the New button

To do this, all we need to do is add all of the customer fields to the search criteria. We can start by creating a new search criteria record.

Click on the **New** button.

Step 2: Update the Field name

We will start off by adding the Account number as a key search field.

Set the Field name to AccountNum.

Step 3: Click on the New button

We will want to continue on and add a couple more fields to search on.

Click on the **New** button.

Step 4: Choose the Field name

We will add the address of the customer as a search option.

Click on the **Field name** dropdown list And choose **Address**.

Step 5: Click on the New button and select the Field name

We will want to also search on the city.

Click on the **New** button and click on the **Field name** dropdown list And select **City**.

Step 6: Click on the New button and update the Field name

We can add the customer's name as an option to search on.

Click on the **New** button and set the **Field name** to **Name**.

Step 7: Click on the New button and choose the Field name

We will also add the zip code as a searchable field.

Click on the **New** button and click on the **Field name** dropdown list And choose **ZipCode**.

Step 8: Click on the New button and choose the Field name

And finally we will add the person that is the primary contact for the customer as a searchable field.

Click on the **New** button and click on the **Field name** dropdown list And choose **ContactPersonId**.

 www.dynamicscompanions.com
Dynamics Companions

- 176 -

www.blindsquirrelpublishing.com
© 2019 Blind Squirrel Publishing, LLC , All Rights Reserved

BLIND SQUIRREL
PUBLISHING

DYNAMICS COMPANIONS
BARE BONES CONFIGURATION GUIDE

CONFIGURING SALES ORDER MANAGEMENT WITHIN DYNAMICS 365 FOR FINANCE & OPERATIONS
MODULE 1: CONFIGURING SALES ORDER MANAGEMENT CONTROLS

Step 9: Click on the Update search data button

There is one more step that we need to perform before the Customer Search will work, and that is to refresh the search data that is cached away.

Click on the **Update search data** button.

Step 10: Click on the Yes button

This will open up a warning message telling you that you are about to change the search which we will want to confirm.

Click on the **Yes** button.

Step 11: Click on the OK button

This will take you to the **Refresh Full Text Search** dialog box, where we are able to confirm that we want to update the customer data.

Click on the **OK** button.

www.dynamicscompanions.com
Dynamics Companions

- 177 -

www.blindsquirrelpublishing.com
© 2019 Blind Squirrel Publishing, LLC , All Rights Reserved

BLIND SQUIRREL
PUBLISHING

DYNAMICS COMPANIONS
BARE BONES CONFIGURATION GUIDE

CONFIGURING SALES ORDER MANAGEMENT WITHIN DYNAMICS 365 FOR FINANCE & OPERATIONS
MODULE 1: CONFIGURING SALES ORDER MANAGEMENT CONTROLS

Configuring the Customer search criteria

How to do it...

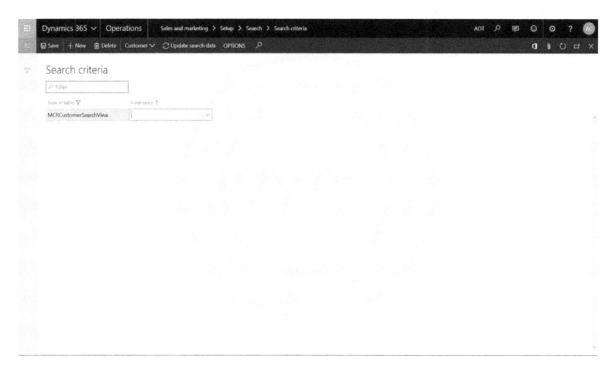

Step 1: Click on the New button

To do this, all we need to do is add all of the customer fields to the search criteria. We can start by creating a new search criteria record.

To do this just click on the **New** button.

DYNAMICS COMPANIONS
BARE BONES CONFIGURATION GUIDE

CONFIGURING SALES ORDER MANAGEMENT WITHIN DYNAMICS 365 FOR FINANCE & OPERATIONS
MODULE 1: CONFIGURING SALES ORDER MANAGEMENT CONTROLS

Configuring the Customer search criteria

How to do it...

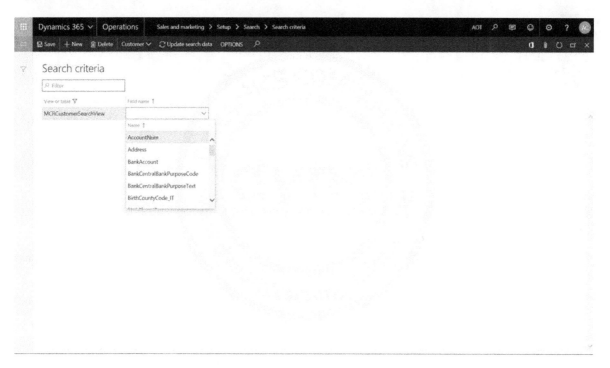

Step 1: Click on the New button

If we click on the **Field Name** dropdown list, we will see all of the different fields that we can search on.

dynᶜ

www.dynamicscompanions.com
Dynamics Companions

- 179 -

www.blindsquirrelpublishing.com
© 2019 Blind Squirrel Publishing, LLC , All Rights Reserved

BLIND SQUIRREL
PUBLISHING

DYNAMICS COMPANIONS
BARE BONES CONFIGURATION GUIDE

CONFIGURING SALES ORDER MANAGEMENT WITHIN DYNAMICS 365 FOR FINANCE & OPERATIONS
MODULE 1: CONFIGURING SALES ORDER MANAGEMENT CONTROLS

Configuring the Customer search criteria

How to do it...

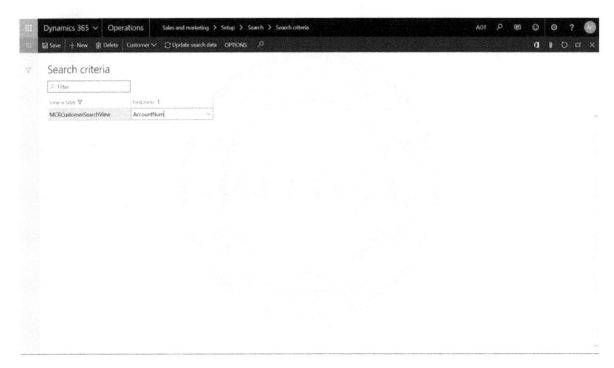

Step 2: Update the Field name

We will start off by adding the Account number as a key search field.

To do this just change the **Field name** value.

This time, we will want to set the **Field name** to **AccountNum**.

www.dynamicscompanions.com
Dynamics Companions

- 180 -

www.blindsquirrelpublishing.com
© 2019 Blind Squirrel Publishing, LLC , All Rights Reserved

BLIND SQUIRREL
PUBLISHING

DYNAMICS COMPANIONS
BARE BONES CONFIGURATION GUIDE

CONFIGURING SALES ORDER MANAGEMENT WITHIN DYNAMICS 365 FOR FINANCE & OPERATIONS
MODULE 1: CONFIGURING SALES ORDER MANAGEMENT CONTROLS

Configuring the Customer search criteria

How to do it...

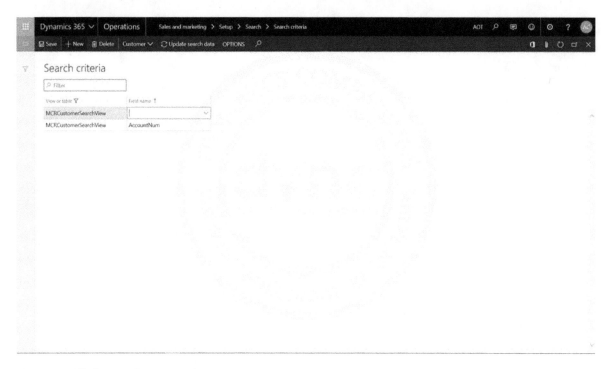

Step 3: Click on the New button

We will want to continue on and add a couple more fields to search on.

To do this all we need to do is click on the **New** button.

www.dynamicscompanions.com
Dynamics Companions

- 181 -

www.blindsquirrelpublishing.com
© 2019 Blind Squirrel Publishing, LLC , All Rights Reserved

BLIND SQUIRREL
PUBLISHING

DYNAMICS COMPANIONS
BARE BONES CONFIGURATION GUIDE

CONFIGURING SALES ORDER MANAGEMENT WITHIN DYNAMICS 365 FOR FINANCE & OPERATIONS
MODULE 1: CONFIGURING SALES ORDER MANAGEMENT CONTROLS

Configuring the Customer search criteria

How to do it...

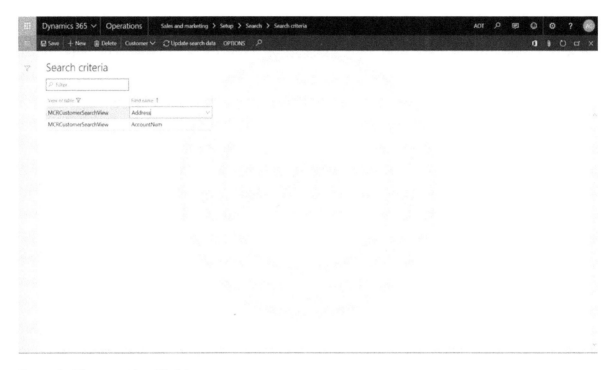

Step 4: Choose the Field name

We will add the address of the customer as a search option.

To do this we will just need to select the **Field name** option from the dropdown list.

For this example, we will want to click on the **Field name** dropdown list and select **Address**.

www.dynamicscompanions.com
Dynamics Companions

- 182 -

www.blindsquirrelpublishing.com
© 2019 Blind Squirrel Publishing, LLC , All Rights Reserved

BLIND SQUIRREL
PUBLISHING

DYNAMICS COMPANIONS
BARE BONES CONFIGURATION GUIDE

CONFIGURING SALES ORDER MANAGEMENT WITHIN DYNAMICS 365 FOR FINANCE & OPERATIONS
MODULE 1: CONFIGURING SALES ORDER MANAGEMENT CONTROLS

Configuring the Customer search criteria

How to do it...

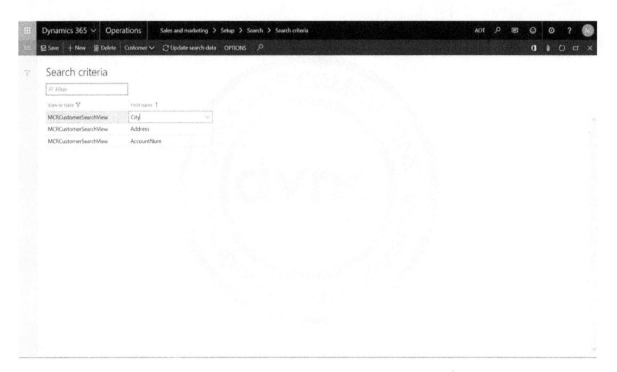

Step 5: Click on the New button and select the Field name

We will want to also search on the city.

To do this all we need to do is click on the **New** button and select the **Field name** value from the dropdown list.

This time, we will want to click on the **Field name** dropdown list and pick **City**.

dyn c
www.dynamicscompanions.com
Dynamics Companions

- 183 -

www.blindsquirrelpublishing.com
© 2019 Blind Squirrel Publishing, LLC , All Rights Reserved

BLIND SQUIRREL
PUBLISHING

DYNAMICS COMPANIONS
BARE BONES CONFIGURATION GUIDE

CONFIGURING SALES ORDER MANAGEMENT WITHIN DYNAMICS 365 FOR FINANCE & OPERATIONS
MODULE 1: CONFIGURING SALES ORDER MANAGEMENT CONTROLS

Configuring the Customer search criteria

How to do it...

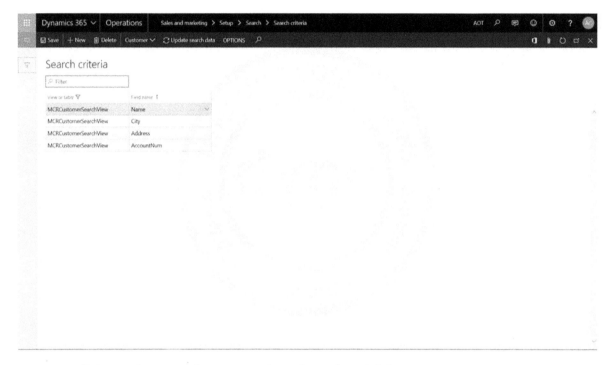

Step 6: Click on the New button and update the Field name

We can add the customer's name as an option to search on.

To do this just click on the **New** button and change the **Field name** value.

This time, we will want to set the **Field name** to **Name**.

www.dynamicscompanions.com
Dynamics Companions

- 184 -

www.blindsquirrelpublishing.com
© 2019 Blind Squirrel Publishing, LLC , All Rights Reserved

BLIND SQUIRREL
PUBLISHING

DYNAMICS COMPANIONS
BARE BONES CONFIGURATION GUIDE

CONFIGURING SALES ORDER MANAGEMENT WITHIN DYNAMICS 365 FOR FINANCE & OPERATIONS
MODULE 1: CONFIGURING SALES ORDER MANAGEMENT CONTROLS

Configuring the Customer search criteria

How to do it...

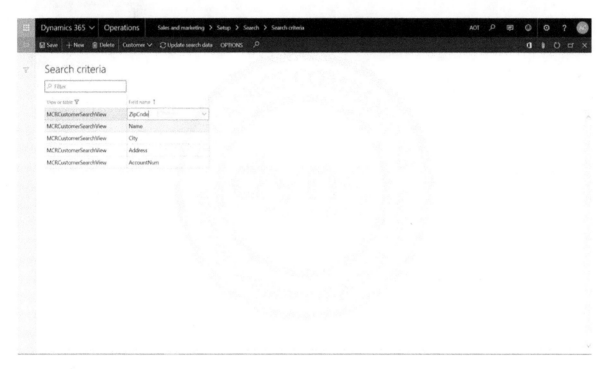

Step 7: Click on the New button and choose the Field name

We will also add the zip code as a searchable field.

To do this just click on the **New** button and pick the **Field name** option from the dropdown list.

This time, we will want to click on the **Field name** dropdown list and pick **ZipCode**.

dyn©
www.dynamicscompanions.com
Dynamics Companions
- 185 -
www.blindsquirrelpublishing.com
© 2019 Blind Squirrel Publishing, LLC , All Rights Reserved
BLIND SQUIRREL
PUBLISHING

DYNAMICS COMPANIONS
BARE BONES CONFIGURATION GUIDE

CONFIGURING SALES ORDER MANAGEMENT WITHIN DYNAMICS 365 FOR FINANCE & OPERATIONS
MODULE 1: CONFIGURING SALES ORDER MANAGEMENT CONTROLS

Configuring the Customer search criteria

How to do it...

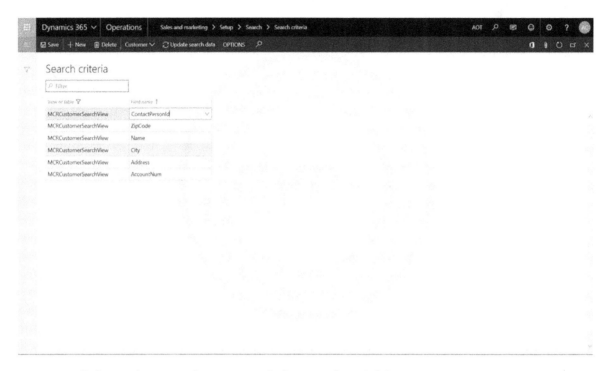

Step 8: Click on the New button and choose the Field name

And finally we will add the person that is the primary contact for the customer as a searchable field.

To do this just click on the **New** button and pick the **Field name** option from the dropdown list.

For this example, we will want to click on the **Field name** dropdown list and select **ContactPersonId**.

www.dynamicscompanions.com
Dynamics Companions

- 186 -

www.blindsquirrelpublishing.com
© 2019 Blind Squirrel Publishing, LLC , All Rights Reserved

BLIND SQUIRREL
PUBLISHING

DYNAMICS COMPANIONS
BARE BONES CONFIGURATION GUIDE

CONFIGURING SALES ORDER MANAGEMENT WITHIN DYNAMICS 365 FOR FINANCE & OPERATIONS
MODULE 1: CONFIGURING SALES ORDER MANAGEMENT CONTROLS

Configuring the Customer search criteria

How to do it...

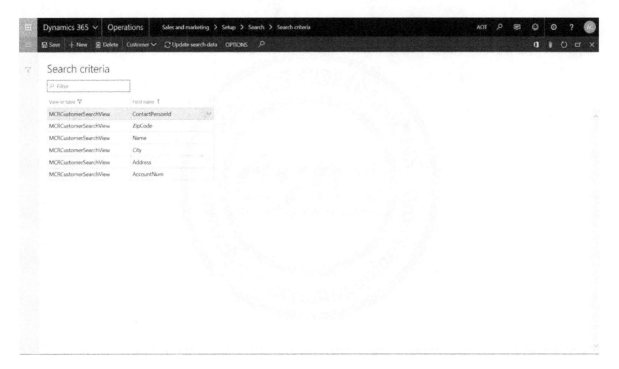

Step 9: Click on the Update search data button

There is one more step that we need to perform before the Customer Search will work, and that is to refresh the search data that is cached away.

To do this all we need to do is click on the **Update search data** button in the menu bar.

DYNAMICS COMPANIONS
BARE BONES CONFIGURATION GUIDE

CONFIGURING SALES ORDER MANAGEMENT WITHIN DYNAMICS 365 FOR FINANCE & OPERATIONS
MODULE 1: CONFIGURING SALES ORDER MANAGEMENT CONTROLS

Configuring the Customer search criteria

How to do it...

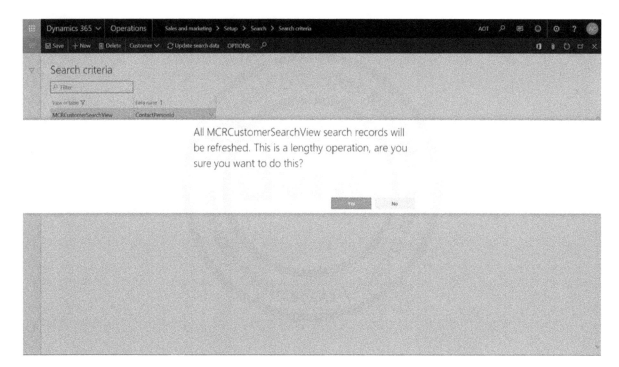

Step 10: Click on the Yes button

This will open up a warning message telling you that you are about to change the search which we will want to confirm.

To do this just click on the **Yes** button.

DYNAMICS COMPANIONS
BARE BONES CONFIGURATION GUIDE

CONFIGURING SALES ORDER MANAGEMENT WITHIN DYNAMICS 365 FOR FINANCE & OPERATIONS
MODULE 1: CONFIGURING SALES ORDER MANAGEMENT CONTROLS

Configuring the Customer search criteria

How to do it...

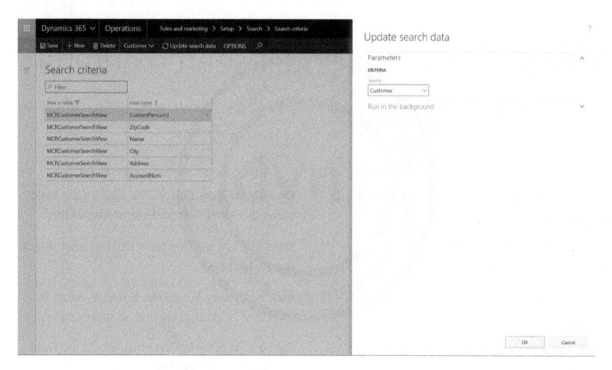

Step 11: Click on the OK button

This will take you to the **Refresh Full Text Search** dialog box, where we are able to confirm that we want to update the customer data.

To do this just click on the **OK** button.

dync
www.dynamicscompanions.com
Dynamics Companions

- 189 -

www.blindsquirrelpublishing.com
© 2019 Blind Squirrel Publishing, LLC, All Rights Reserved

BLIND SQUIRREL
PUBLISHING

DYNAMICS COMPANIONS
BARE BONES CONFIGURATION GUIDE

CONFIGURING SALES ORDER MANAGEMENT WITHIN DYNAMICS 365 FOR FINANCE & OPERATIONS
MODULE 1: CONFIGURING SALES ORDER MANAGEMENT CONTROLS

Configuring the Product search criteria

Now that we have set up the customer search criteria we will want to also set up the criteria that we will want to use when we are searching for products.

How to do it...

Step 1: Click on the Customer button and click on the Product button

We can do this by switching to the Product option within this form.

Click on the **Customer** button and click on the **Product** button.

Step 2: Click on the New button and select the Field name

Let's start by adding a search field for alternate product identifiers.

Click on the **New** button and click on the **Field name** dropdown list And choose **AltItemId**.

Step 3: Click on the New button and select the Field name

Next we will add a search option for the items identifier.

Click on the **New** button and click on the **Field name** dropdown list And select **ItemId**.

Step 4: Click on the New button and select the Field name

We will add the alias name field that we have associated with the product as well.

Click on the **New** button and click on the **Field name** dropdown list And select **NameAlias**.

Step 5: Click on the New button and select the Field name

And finally we will add the products name to the list of fields that we will be searching on.

Click on the **New** button and click on the **Field name** dropdown list And choose **ProductName**.

Step 6: Click on the Update search data button

Just like with the customers, we will also need to update the search data to incorporate all of these fields that we have specified for the product search.

Click on the **Update search data** button.

Step 7: Click on the Yes button

This will open up a confirmation dialog box asking us if we want to really update the search data, which we will want to do.

Click on the **Yes** button.

Step 8: Click on the OK button

When the **Refresh Full Text Search** dialog box is displayed to allow us to start the update

 www.dynamicscompanions.com
Dynamics Companions

- 190 -

www.blindsquirrelpublishing.com
© 2019 Blind Squirrel Publishing, LLC, All Rights Reserved

BLIND SQUIRREL
PUBLISHING

DYNAMICS COMPANIONS
BARE BONES CONFIGURATION GUIDE

CONFIGURING SALES ORDER MANAGEMENT WITHIN DYNAMICS 365 FOR FINANCE & OPERATIONS
MODULE 1: CONFIGURING SALES ORDER MANAGEMENT CONTROLS

process for the search data. Make sure that the **Source** field is set to **Products** before confirming the update.

Click on the **OK** button.

www.dynamicscompanions.com
Dynamics Companions

- 191 -

www.blindsquirrelpublishing.com
© 2019 Blind Squirrel Publishing, LLC , All Rights Reserved

BLIND SQUIRREL
PUBLISHING

DYNAMICS COMPANIONS
BARE BONES CONFIGURATION GUIDE

CONFIGURING SALES ORDER MANAGEMENT WITHIN DYNAMICS 365 FOR FINANCE & OPERATIONS
MODULE 1: CONFIGURING SALES ORDER MANAGEMENT CONTROLS

Configuring the Product search criteria

How to do it...

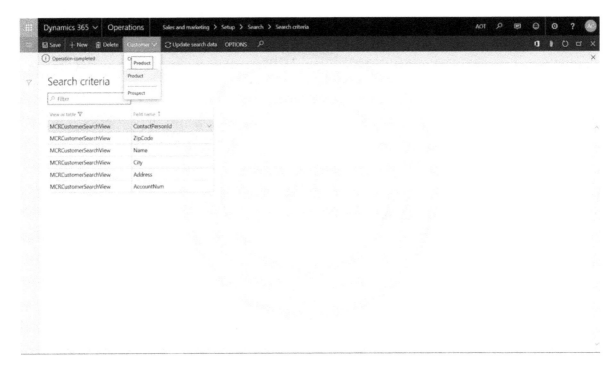

Step 1: Click on the Customer button and click on the Product button

We can do this by switching to the Product option within this form.

We can do this by switching to the Product option within this form.

dyn c
Dynamics Companions

www.dynamicscompanions.com
Dynamics Companions

- 192 -

www.blindsquirrelpublishing.com
© 2019 Blind Squirrel Publishing, LLC , All Rights Reserved

BLIND SQUIRREL
PUBLISHING

DYNAMICS COMPANIONS
BARE BONES CONFIGURATION GUIDE

CONFIGURING SALES ORDER MANAGEMENT WITHIN DYNAMICS 365 FOR FINANCE & OPERATIONS
MODULE 1: CONFIGURING SALES ORDER MANAGEMENT CONTROLS

Configuring the Product search criteria

How to do it...

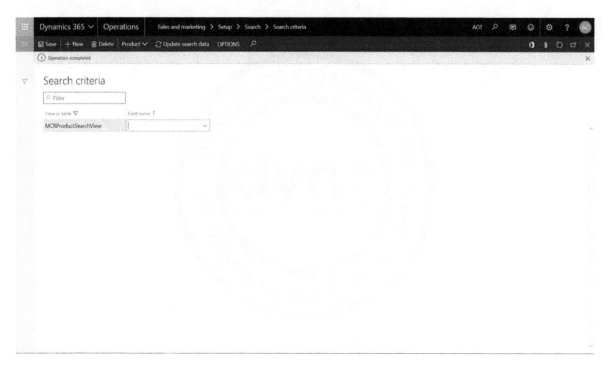

Step 1: Click on the Customer button and click on the Product button

This will switch the form to be the **Product** view of the search criteria which is empty right now.

www.dynamicscompanions.com
Dynamics Companions

- 193 -

www.blindsquirrelpublishing.com
© 2019 Blind Squirrel Publishing, LLC , All Rights Reserved

BLIND SQUIRREL
PUBLISHING

DYNAMICS COMPANIONS
BARE BONES CONFIGURATION GUIDE

CONFIGURING SALES ORDER MANAGEMENT WITHIN DYNAMICS 365 FOR FINANCE & OPERATIONS
MODULE 1: CONFIGURING SALES ORDER MANAGEMENT CONTROLS

Configuring the Product search criteria

How to do it...

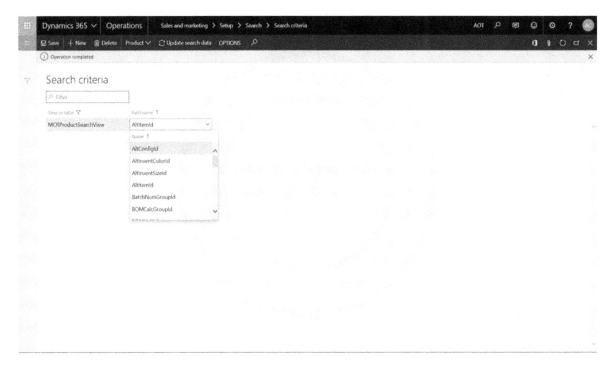

Step 2: Click on the New button and select the Field name

Let's start by adding a search field for alternate product identifiers.

To do this just click on the **New** button and pick the **Field name** option from the dropdown list.

For this example, we will want to click on the **Field name** dropdown list and pick **AltItemId**.

DYNAMICS COMPANIONS
BARE BONES CONFIGURATION GUIDE

CONFIGURING SALES ORDER MANAGEMENT WITHIN DYNAMICS 365 FOR FINANCE & OPERATIONS
MODULE 1: CONFIGURING SALES ORDER MANAGEMENT CONTROLS

Configuring the Product search criteria

How to do it...

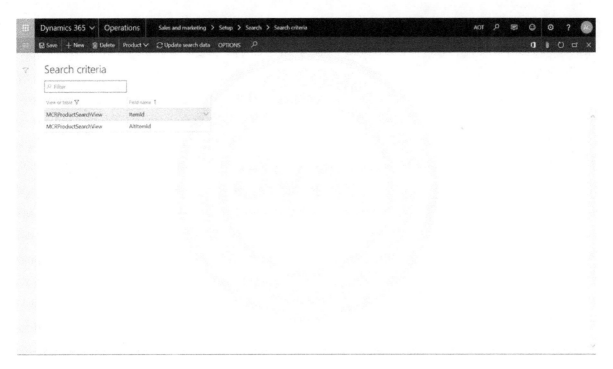

Step 3: Click on the New button and select the Field name

Next we will add a search option for the items identifier.

To do this all we need to do is click on the **New** button and select the **Field name** value from the dropdown list.

This time, we will want to click on the **Field name** dropdown list and select **ItemId**.

dyn c

www.dynamicscompanions.com
Dynamics Companions

- 195 -

www.blindsquirrelpublishing.com
© 2019 Blind Squirrel Publishing, LLC , All Rights Reserved

BLIND SQUIRREL
PUBLISHING

DYNAMICS COMPANIONS
BARE BONES CONFIGURATION GUIDE

CONFIGURING SALES ORDER MANAGEMENT WITHIN DYNAMICS 365 FOR FINANCE & OPERATIONS
MODULE 1: CONFIGURING SALES ORDER MANAGEMENT CONTROLS

Configuring the Product search criteria

How to do it...

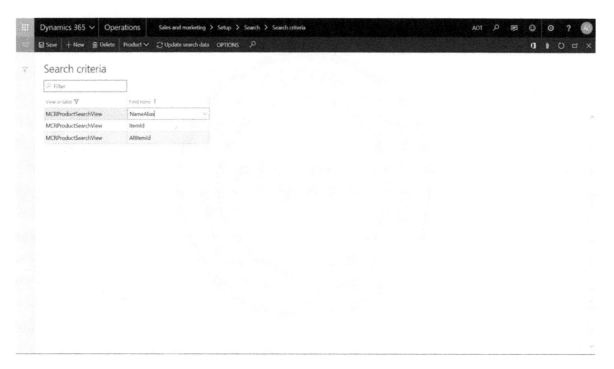

Step 4: Click on the New button and select the Field name

We will add the alias name field that we have associated with the product as well.

To do this all we need to do is click on the **New** button and pick the **Field name** value from the dropdown list.

For this example, we will want to click on the **Field name** dropdown list and pick **NameAlias**.

dync
www.dynamicscompanions.com
Dynamics Companions

- 196 -

www.blindsquirrelpublishing.com
© 2019 Blind Squirrel Publishing, LLC , All Rights Reserved

BLIND SQUIRREL
PUBLISHING

DYNAMICS COMPANIONS
BARE BONES CONFIGURATION GUIDE

CONFIGURING SALES ORDER MANAGEMENT WITHIN DYNAMICS 365 FOR FINANCE & OPERATIONS
MODULE 1: CONFIGURING SALES ORDER MANAGEMENT CONTROLS

Configuring the Product search criteria

How to do it...

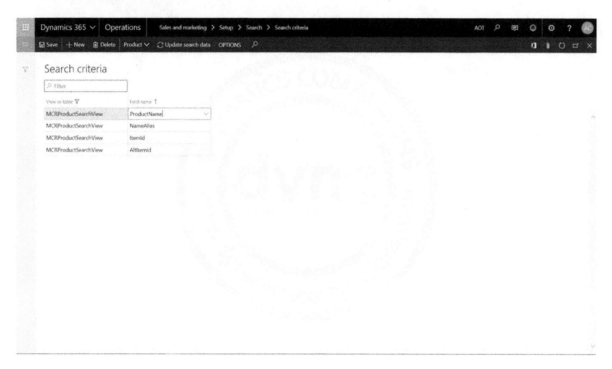

Step 5: Click on the New button and select the Field name

And finally we will add the products name to the list of fields that we will be searching on.

To do this all we need to do is click on the **New** button and select the **Field name** value from the dropdown list.

This time, we will want to click on the **Field name** dropdown list and select **ProductName**.

www.dynamicscompanions.com
Dynamics Companions

- 197 -

www.blindsquirrelpublishing.com
© 2019 Blind Squirrel Publishing, LLC , All Rights Reserved

BLIND SQUIRREL
PUBLISHING

DYNAMICS COMPANIONS
BARE BONES CONFIGURATION GUIDE

CONFIGURING SALES ORDER MANAGEMENT WITHIN DYNAMICS 365 FOR FINANCE & OPERATIONS
MODULE 1: CONFIGURING SALES ORDER MANAGEMENT CONTROLS

Configuring the Product search criteria

How to do it...

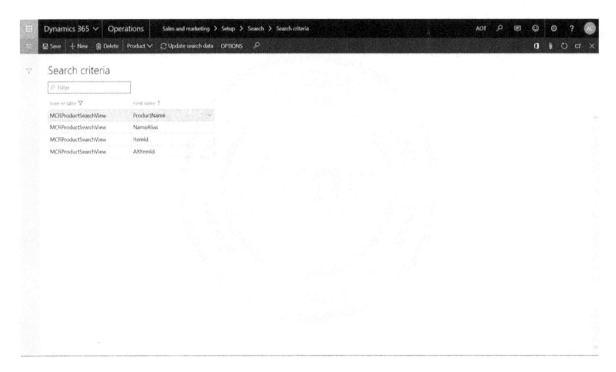

Step 6: Click on the Update search data button

Just like with the customers, we will also need to update the search data to incorporate all of these fields that we have specified for the product search.

To do this just click on the **Update search data** button in the menu bar.

www.dynamicscompanions.com
Dynamics Companions

- 198 -

www.blindsquirrelpublishing.com
© 2019 Blind Squirrel Publishing, LLC , All Rights Reserved

BLIND SQUIRREL
PUBLISHING

DYNAMICS COMPANIONS
BARE BONES CONFIGURATION GUIDE

CONFIGURING SALES ORDER MANAGEMENT WITHIN DYNAMICS 365 FOR FINANCE & OPERATIONS
MODULE 1: CONFIGURING SALES ORDER MANAGEMENT CONTROLS

Configuring the Product search criteria

How to do it...

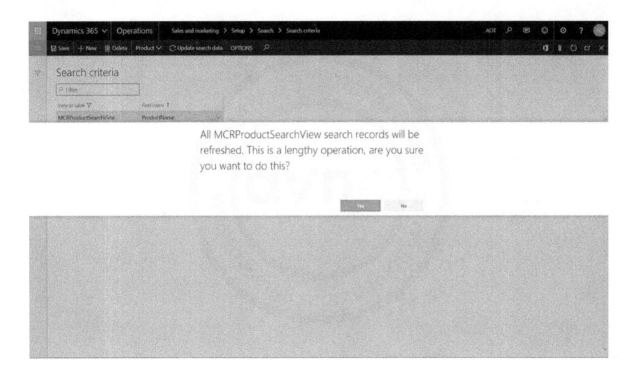

Step 7: Click on the Yes button

This will open up a confirmation dialog box asking us if we want to really update the search data, which we will want to do.

To do this just click on the **Yes** button.

dyn c

www.dynamicscompanions.com
Dynamics Companions

- 199 -

www.blindsquirrelpublishing.com
© 2019 Blind Squirrel Publishing, LLC , All Rights Reserved

BLIND SQUIRREL
PUBLISHING

DYNAMICS COMPANIONS
BARE BONES CONFIGURATION GUIDE

CONFIGURING SALES ORDER MANAGEMENT WITHIN DYNAMICS 365 FOR FINANCE & OPERATIONS
MODULE 1: CONFIGURING SALES ORDER MANAGEMENT CONTROLS

Configuring the Product search criteria

How to do it...

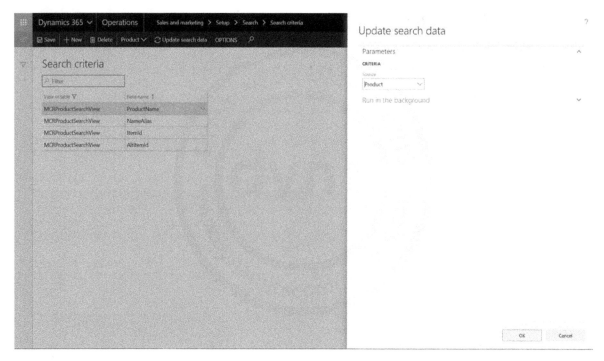

Step 8: Click on the OK button

When the **Refresh Full Text Search** dialog box is displayed to allow us to start the update process for the search data. Make sure that the **Source** field is set to **Products** before confirming the update.

To do this just click on the **OK** button.

www.dynamicscompanions.com
Dynamics Companions

- 200 -

www.blindsquirrelpublishing.com
© 2019 Blind Squirrel Publishing, LLC , All Rights Reserved

BLIND SQUIRREL
PUBLISHING

DYNAMICS COMPANIONS
BARE BONES CONFIGURATION GUIDE

CONFIGURING SALES ORDER MANAGEMENT WITHIN DYNAMICS 365 FOR FINANCE & OPERATIONS
MODULE 1: CONFIGURING SALES ORDER MANAGEMENT CONTROLS

Configuring the Product search criteria

How to do it...

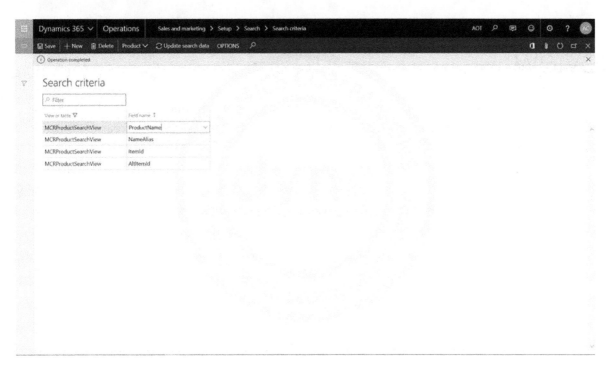

Step 8: Click on the OK button

After you have done that you can just exit from the form.

dyn⊃
www.dynamicscompanions.com
Dynamics Companions

- 201 -

www.blindsquirrelpublishing.com
© 2019 Blind Squirrel Publishing, LLC , All Rights Reserved

BLIND SQUIRREL
PUBLISHING

DYNAMICS COMPANIONS
BARE BONES CONFIGURATION GUIDE

CONFIGURING SALES ORDER MANAGEMENT WITHIN DYNAMICS 365 FOR FINANCE & OPERATIONS
MODULE 1: CONFIGURING SALES ORDER MANAGEMENT CONTROLS

Review

How cool is that. We have just configured the advanced customer and product search within the Sales order area within the system and added some additional criteria that we will want to search through our products and customers with.

DYNAMICS COMPANIONS
BARE BONES CONFIGURATION GUIDE

CONFIGURING SALES ORDER MANAGEMENT WITHIN DYNAMICS 365 FOR FINANCE & OPERATIONS
MODULE 1: CONFIGURING SALES ORDER MANAGEMENT CONTROLS

Summary

Congratulations. You have just finished setting up all of the basic codes and controls that we will need in order to start using the Sales order processing feature within the system.

You have configure the basic codes that you will need, and also some of the mechanics around the order process like event tracking and also the search feature.

Now that we have done the legwork here we can start looking at the transactions and how the sales order processing feature flows within Dynamics 365.

dyn

www.dynamicscompanions.com
Dynamics Companions

- 203 -

www.blindsquirrelpublishing.com
© 2019 Blind Squirrel Publishing, LLC , All Rights Reserved

BLIND SQUIRREL
PUBLISHING

DYNAMICS COMPANIONS
BARE BONES CONFIGURATION GUIDE

CONFIGURING SALES ORDER MANAGEMENT WITHIN DYNAMICS 365 FOR FINANCE & OPERATIONS
MODULE 1: CONFIGURING SALES ORDER MANAGEMENT CONTROLS

About The Author

Murray Fife is an Author of over 20 books on Microsoft Dynamics including the Bare Bones Configuration Guide series. These guides comprise of over 15 books which step you through the setup and configuration of Microsoft Dynamics including Finance, Operations, Human Resources, Production, Service Management, and Project Accounting.

Throughout his 25+ years of experience in the software industry he has worked in many different roles during his career, including as a developer, an implementation consultant, a trainer and a demo guy within the partner channel which gives him a great understanding of the requirements for both customers and partners perspective.

If you are interested in contacting Murray or want to follow his blogs and posts then here is all of his contact information:

Email:	murray@murrayfife.com
Twitter:	@murrayfife
Facebook:	facebook.com/murraycfife
Google:	google.com/+murrayfife
LinkedIn:	linkedin.com/in/murrayfife
Blog:	atinkerersnotebook.com
Slideshare:	slideshare.net/murrayfife
Amazon:	amazon.com/author/murrayfife

www.dynamicscompanions.com
Dynamics Companions

- 205 -

www.blindsquirrelpublishing.com
© 2019 Blind Squirrel Publishing, LLC , All Rights Reserved

BLIND SQUIRREL
PUBLISHING

DYNAMICS COMPANIONS
BARE BONES CONFIGURATION GUIDE

CONFIGURING SALES ORDER MANAGEMENT WITHIN DYNAMICS 365 FOR FINANCE & OPERATIONS
MODULE 1: CONFIGURING SALES ORDER MANAGEMENT CONTROLS

Need More Help with Microsoft Dynamics AX 2012 or Dynamics 365 for Operations

We are firm believers that Microsoft Dynamics AX 2012 or Dynamics 365 is not a hard product to learn, but the problem is where do you start. Which is why we developed the Bare Bones Configuration Guides. The aim of this series is to step you though the configuration of Microsoft Dynamics from a blank system, and then step you through the setup of all of the core modules within Microsoft Dynamics. We start with the setup of a base system, then move on to the financial, distribution, and operations modules.

Each book builds upon the previous ones, and by the time you have worked through all of the guides then you will have completely configured a simple (but functional) Microsoft Dynamics instance. To make it even more worthwhile you will have a far better understanding of Microsoft Dynamics and also how everything fits together.

As of now there are 16 guides in this series broken out as follows:

- Configuring a Training Environment
- Configuring an Organization
- Configuring the General Ledger
- Configuring Cash and Bank Management
- Configuring Accounts Receivable
- Configuring Accounts Payable
- Configuring Product Information Management
- Configuring Inventory Management

- Configuring Procurement and Sourcing
- Configuring Sales Order Management
- Configuring Human Resource Management
- Configuring Project Management and Accounting
- Configuring Production Control
- Configuring Sales and Marketing
- Configuring Service Management
- Configuring Warehouse Management

Although you can get each of these guides individually, and we think that each one is a great Visual resources to step you through each of the particular modules, for those of you that want to take full advantage of the series, you will want to start from the beginning and work through them one by one. After you have done that you would have done people told me was impossible for one persons to do, and that is to configure all of the core modules within Microsoft Dynamics.

If you are interested in finding out more about the series and also view all of the details including topics covered within the module, then browse to the Bare Bones Configuration Guide landing page on the Microsoft Dynamics Companions website. You will find all of the details, and also downloadable resources that help you with the setup of Microsoft Dynamics. Here is the full link: http://www.dynamicscompanions.com/